DATE DUE			

—P E O P L E   T O   K N O W—

ALICE WALKER

Author of
The Color Purple

Barbara Kramer

Enslow Publishers, Inc.

40 Industrial Road	PO Box 38
Box 398	Aldershot
Berkeley Heights, NJ 07922	Hants GU12 6BP
USA	UK

http://www.enslow.com

Library of Congress Cataloging-in-Publication Data

Kramer, Barbara.
    Alice Walker: author of *The Color Purple* / Barbara Kramer.
        p. cm. — (People to know)
    Includes bibliographical references and index.
    Summary: Describes the life of the author and activist, from her childhood in
Georgia to her emergence as a subject of both adulation and controversy.
    ISBN 0-89490-620-8
    1. Walker, Alice, 1944—Biography—Juvenile literature. 2. Afro-American
women authors—Biography—Juvenile literature. 3. Afro-American women civil
rights workers—Biography—Juvenile literature. [1. Walker, Alice, 1944- .
2. Authors, American. 3. Civil rights workers. 4.Afro-Americans—
Biography. 5. Women—Biography.] I. Title. II. Series.
PS3573.A425Z75 1995
813'.54—dc20   95-5809
[B]   CIP
                                                        AC
Printed in the United States of America

10 9 8 7 6 5

Illustration Credits:
Courtesy of the family of Alice Walker, pp. 17, 49; ©Flip Schulke, p. 33;
© Jean Weisinger, pp. 4, 104, 108; John Peck, pp. 19, 27; L.A. Hyder, pp.
77, 83; Movie Still Archives, pp. 10, 92; Reproduced through the courtesy
of Joseph Solomon, representing the estate of Carl Van Vechten, from the
collection of the Cedar Rapids Community School District, p. 57; Robert
Allen, pp. 95, 97; Sarah Lawrence College Archives, p. 37; Sloan
Gregory/ *The Eatonton Messenger*, p. 7; Spelman College Archives, pp. 31,
43; Wellesley College Archives, p. 61.

Cover Illustration:
© Jean Weisinger

Contents

1 "Welcome Home!" 5

2 "It Was Great Fun Being Cute!" 13

3 Confidence Returns 23

4 "To Hell With Dying" 29

5 "The Stories Are Knee-Deep" 41

6 Zora 53

7 "Revolutionary Petunias" 63

8 *The Color Purple* 73

9 Changes 85

10 A Delicate Subject 101

Chronology 112

Chapter Notes 114

Further Reading 124

Index 126

Alice Walker

1

"Welcome Home!"

One by one, limousines pulled up to the entrance of the Pex Theater. Cameras flashed as guests, dressed in their finest evening attire, stepped onto the red carpet that had been rolled out for the occasion. Two huge searchlights scanned the sky. Their beams crisscrossed at their highest points above the theater.

Purple was in evidence everywhere—purple shoes, purple dresses, and even purple lipstick. The inside of the Pex Theater was decorated with beautiful purple flowers.

The fanfare was for premiere night—January 18, 1986. But the location was not Hollywood, California. It was 'Eatonton, Georgia—the hometown of Alice Walker, author of the award-winning novel *The Color*

Purple. More than one thousand friends, family, and fans turned out for two showings of the movie based on that novel.

As a child growing up in Eatonton, Alice stood outside the corner drugstore on hot summer afternoons. Through the window, she peered at the white children who were seated on stools, drinking sodas and eating ice cream cones in air-conditioned comfort. African Americans were allowed inside the store to buy items, but any food that they wanted had to be eaten outside.

More than thirty years later, for the premiere, the downtown merchants decorated their windows with purple crepe paper. There was a large banner with the words "Welcome Home, Alice Walker" written across it in big bold letters. Tickets for the premiere sold for $10 each. The proceeds went to *The Color Purple* Scholarship Fund.

The festivities were organized by Walker's sister Ruth Walker Hood. She got the idea while attending the premiere for the movie in New York City. "I wanted to honor her now. Not wait until she was dead and they named some street after her," Hood told reporters.[1]

Before the second showing of the movie, Walker rose to address the audience. With her large brown eyes she scanned the waiting faces. Then she began to speak in her gentle manner.

"I think of this movie as a gift to you. . . . I hope that when you open this present you won't be distracted by

At Eatonton's premiere for *The Color Purple*, Superintendent of Schools Bill Dabbs proclaimed January 13-18 as "Alice Walker Week" in Putnam County. Walker's sister, Ruth Walker Hood (right), joined Walker and Dabbs on the speaker's platform.

what people say about the ribbon and the wrapping paper."[2] Her remarks were an obvious reference to the controversy the book, and now the movie, had created.

The Color Purple tells the story of Celie, an uneducated African-American woman growing up in the South in the early 1920s–1940s. The book is a series of letters written by Celie and her sister Nettie.

In letters to God, Celie writes about the repeated rapes by her stepfather, followed by her marriage to a man so cruel that she can't bring herself to call him by name. Although others call him Albert, she refers to him in her letters as Mr._____.

When her husband's mistress Shug Avery becomes ill, he brings Shug into his home and forces Celie to take care of her. At first Shug is mean to Celie, but eventually they come to love each other. Through her relationship with Shug, Celie becomes more self-sufficient. Finally she is able to stand up to her husband.

The book, published in June 1982, was on *The New York Times* best-seller list for over twenty-five weeks. It won the American Book Award and the Pulitzer prize—the most important award given to American writers. Alice Walker was the first African-American woman to receive that honor in the fiction category.

Newsweek magazine hailed *The Color Purple* as "an American novel of permanent importance."[3] *The New Yorker* praised it as "fiction of the highest order."[4]

There was also negative criticism, however. After all, *The Color Purple* discussed controversial issues such as rape, incest, wife-beating, lesbianism, drugs, murder, alcoholism, and African tribal customs. Walker expected some opposition, but what shocked her was the reaction from some African-American men.[5] They felt that she had portrayed all African-American men as "cruel" and "abusive," and the women as "noble" and "long-suffering."

Earl Caldwell, a columnist for the *New York Daily News*, wrote, "*The Color Purple* can make you see red. That's especially true if you are a man and happen to be black."[6]

The Los Angeles, California, opening of the movie was marred by picketers. They carried signs reading, "Are white producers trying to destroy black men?"[7]

Critics were especially angry about the character of "Mister," Celie's husband. They thought African-American men were too often shown as being abusive. They felt that it was time films showed African-American males as positive role models.

In the movie, actor Danny Glover played the role of "Mister." He was not offended by the part. "Mister was an adequate representation of one particular story," he said. "He's a product of his past and his present and I think we showed that he has some capabilities for changing. It was a complex multidimensional role."[8]

Actress Oprah Winfrey was also in the movie. She won an Oscar nomination for her role as Sophia, the

Danny Glover played the role of "Mister" in the movie *The Color Purple*. It was a character many people criticized.

wife of Celie's stepson. She agreed with Glover. "The movie is not meant to represent black people or black men," she said. "It's one woman's story."[9]

However, Walker learned that she had actually written a story for many women. Because of *The Color Purple,* she received letters from abused children and women from all over the world. They wrote that they identified with Celie and that her courage gave them hope.

In June 1983, Alice traveled to China with a group of twelve American women writers. There she was told by an editor of a Shanghai literary magazine that *The Color Purple* was being translated into Chinese. "But, Alice, it is a very *Chinese* story," the editor said.[10]

The controversy surrounding *The Color Purple* did not discourage Walker. She would continue to write in her straightforward fashion about the people she knew and the issues she cared about.

2

"It Was Great Fun Being Cute!"

Alice Walker was born in Eatonton, Georgia, on February 9, 1944. She was the youngest of eight children. The midwife charged three dollars for helping with the delivery. It was the first time Alice's father had been able to pay cash. With the births of his other children, he had given the midwife a pig in return for her services.

Alice's father Willie Lee Walker earned about $300 a year from sharecropping and dairy farming. He worked long hard days in the fields, never once having a vacation.

The family moved often, going from one landowner to another. Alice Walker remembers the landowners as "evil greedy men."[1] The housing was always cramped and shabby—small shacks with leaky roofs that were cold in the winter and hot in the summer. For Alice, the bright spot in these living conditions was her mother's flowers.[2]

Her mother Minnie Tallulah (Lou) Walker ran away from home at the age of seventeen to get married. By the time she was twenty, she already had two children and another one on the way.

Minnie Walker helped in the fields and sometimes added to the family income by working as a maid. She sewed clothes for her family, and canned fruits and vegetables from her garden. In the evenings she made quilts to keep the family warm through the winter.

But somehow she still managed to find the energy for her flowers. She worked early in the mornings before she went out to the fields and again at night until it was too dark to see. She planted flowers everywhere—over fifty varieties.

In a 1991 interview with Alvin P. Sanoff of *U.S. News & World Report*, Alice Walker said:

> I couldn't move anywhere without my eye hitting flowers. So, on the one hand, there was this awful system of exploitation, drudgery and broken spirits and, on the other, this incredibly sustaining natural beauty. I was shortchanged by society, but abundantly fed by nature.[3]

Minnie Walker had a temper, but rarely showed it. Alice did see her get angry when the white landowner suggested that she take her children out of school and put them to work in the fields. Mrs. Walker stood toe to toe with the landowner and said, "Every one of my children will go to school."[4] She had left school in the fourth grade to go to work in the fields. She knew that if her children were to have a better life, they needed a good education.

To Alice Walker, it seemed almost as though their family had two different fathers. One was the man who was father to the oldest four children, and the other was father to the youngest four children.

The older children remembered their father as young and healthy. He had been active in both politics and education. He was one of the first African-American men to vote in Eatonton, and he had helped organize the sharecroppers so that they would not always be at the mercy of the landowners. He had also been a leading supporter of the local one-room African-American school.

The father Alice and the younger children knew had been worn down by cruel landowners and the sharecropping system. He was overweight, and suffered from high blood pressure and diabetes. He seemed distrustful of politics and education.[5] "And why not?" Walker later wrote. "Though he risked his life and livelihood to vote more than once, nothing much changed in his world. Cotton prices continued low. Dairying was hard. White men and women continued to run things, badly."[6]

"Education merely seemed to make his children more critical of him,"[7] Walker wrote. He was good at math, but he too had been forced to quit school to go to work in the fields. As his children became better educated, the separation between the generations appeared to grow larger.

It was Alice's father who first taught her the importance of telling the truth. She was about three years old at the time. Her father questioned her about a broken vase. Alice did not know how to answer. She *had* broken the vase, but she did not know if she should tell him. If she confessed, she might be punished. Or she could say "No" and hope he never found out the truth. Finally she chose to admit her guilt. He did not punish her. In fact, he seemed pleased that she had been honest. From that time on, Alice decided she would always take a chance with the truth.

Alice started school when she was four. In spite of her young age, she was put in the first grade. Her teacher was a kind woman, and Alice did well under her guidance.[8]

When she was six, Alice was to recite for the Easter church service. Other children would be performing too, but her speech was the longest. She was not afraid. She loved to recite and always tried to give it "flourish."[9]

Her sister Ruth had made her a "green, flocked, scalloped-hem dress"[10] for the occasion. She wore shiny patent-leather shoes and white laced anklets.

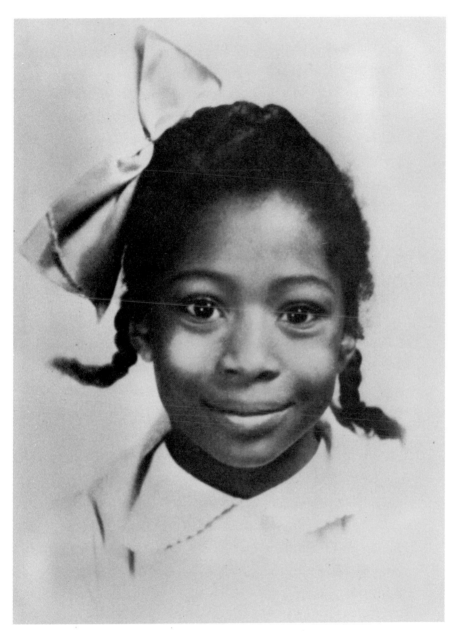

Alice Walker was a happy, outgoing child.

When it was her turn, Alice took her place at the front of the church. Everyone was quiet as she began. She spoke with spirit. Some of the older women called it sassiness, but Alice knew they approved. Her performance was flawless. As she returned to her seat, Alice could hear praises such as "beautiful" and "cute."

Looking back on that time she wrote: "It was great fun being cute. But then one day it ended."[11] That was the day an accident left her blind in one eye.

On Saturday nights, Alice's two youngest brothers and her mother liked to go to the movies. Alice also went along. Westerns were their favorite. They watched cowboys such as Tom Mix, Hopalong Cassidy, and Lash LaRue as they rode, shot, and sang their way through adventures. By the end of the movie the stars had captured the "bad guys" and won the heart of the damsel in distress. The rest of the week her brothers lived out their western fantasies playing cowboys and Indians. Alice, who was a bit of a tomboy, played with them.

One Christmas, Alice's parents gave the boys BB guns. Alice wasn't allowed to have one because she was a girl. From that time on, she had to play the role of the Indian. With her bow and arrows, she did her best to keep up with her brothers while they ran and shot their shiny new guns.

On the day of the accident Alice was standing on top of what served as the family's garage. It really was only "pieces of tin nailed across some poles."[12] Suddenly she

Wards Chapel, in Eatonton, Georgia, was the church where Alice Walker's family worshipped for over one hundred years. It was where she recited as a child.

felt a sharp pain in her right eye. She looked up to see her brother lower his gun. Then both of her brothers ran to her side.

At the time of the accident, her brothers were ten and twelve years old, and Alice was eight. Her brothers pleaded with her not to tell their parents what really happened, knowing that they would be punished. Her older brother found a piece of wire and said, "Say you stepped on one end of it and the other flew up and hit you."[13]

Alice's eye got infected. Her parents nursed her through the next few days as she fought fever and chills. They did finally learn the truth about what happened and took her to the doctor. But that was a week after the accident. The doctor said that she would eventually lose the sight in her other eye too. He was wrong, but for years Alice feared this would happen.[14]

Because of the delay in getting to the doctor, Alice's eye was disfigured with a glob of white scar tissue. It made her feel ugly. The confident little girl who loved to perform, became a shy lonely child. "I used to pray every night that I would wake up and somehow it would be gone," Walker told an interviewer. "I couldn't look at people directly because I thought I was ugly."[15]

The Walkers were living in a new community at that time. The school she attended was in an old prison. On the second floor was a large circle where the electric chair had once sat. Many nights Alice had nightmares about that chair. During the day she was teased about her eye by the other students.

Alice's parents finally decided that it would be better for her to be in her old community, with her old friends. They sent her back to live with her grandparents. But for Alice, it seemed that she was being punished for the accident. It had been her brother's fault, yet she was the one who was sent away.[16]

The accident was a turning point in Alice's life. It was then that she really began to watch people and notice relationships. She spent more time reading and just being alone.

Alice stayed with her grandparents for a year. Then she moved back home. She found it hard to find privacy in her parents' small house with her brothers and sisters around. So Alice began to spend more and more time outdoors. The family did not have indoor plumbing, so even a trip to the spring to get water was a time to be alone.

Like most children, Alice thought about various careers. At one time she wanted to be a scientist because she felt that they helped people.[17] Then she wanted to play the piano. For a while she did take lessons, at fifty cents each. Alice had to earn the money herself by selling eggs. She continued taking lessons as long as she could—until there weren't enough eggs to sell. Then Alice had to give up the lessons.

She also thought about being an artist, but finally decided to be a writer because the supplies were cheaper. Her parents were both wonderful storytellers, and Walker began to write down their stories. She also wrote poems.

Alice kept all her writing in a notebook. She even wrote a preface thanking everyone who was "forced to hear this material—my mother, my teacher, my blind Uncle Frank."[18] Alice soon discovered that writing made her feel a little less lonely.

3

Confidence Returns

Alice had the scar tissue removed from her eye when she was fourteen years old. She was spending the summer in Boston, babysitting with her brother Bill's children. He was older than the brothers Alice had been playing with on the day of the accident. He saw that she suffered embarrassment because of her eye. That summer he paid for the surgery that left only a small "bluish crater"[1] where the scar tissue had been.

After the surgery, Alice's life changed again. Her earlier confidence began to return. She was no longer afraid to look people in the eye. She had always been a good student, but now she was not worried about drawing attention to herself. She participated in class discussions, and her grades improved. By the time that she graduated from high school, she was valedictorian of her class.

Alice was seventeen, a senior in high school, when she first got caught up in the Civil Rights Movement in 1960. Her family had just bought their first television set. They got it so that her mother could watch soap operas. Her mother saw the afternoon shows at the house where she worked as a maid. She wanted to be able to follow the stories on her days off as well. The first African-American face Alice saw on their television screen was Dr. Martin Luther King, Jr., a leader in the Civil Rights Movement.

African Americans had been granted equal rights after the Civil War. However, their equality had not been widely accepted. Blacks were not allowed to attend white schools. They were not served in some restaurants, hotels, and other businesses. African Americans were kept from voting, in some cases, by unlawful literacy tests and poll taxes. They also faced discrimination in renting apartments and buying houses.

Dr. King got involved in the struggle for equal rights in 1955, when he protested the segregated bus system in Montgomery, Alabama. There, a city law ordered blacks to give up their seats on a bus if a white person wanted to sit in that seat or in the same row as that seat.

The city law was challenged when a woman named Rosa Parks refused to give up her seat. She had not planned to start a protest. She was simply tired and wanted to remain seated. Instead she was arrested.

Other African Americans showed their support by boycotting the city buses. To run the boycott, African-American leaders formed an organization called the Montgomery Improvement Association. They asked King to be president of the group.

The boycott lasted a year. It ended on December 20, 1956, with a ruling by the U.S. Supreme Court. The Court forced Montgomery to provide equal seating on buses. The success of the boycott brought King national recognition. He became a leader in the fight against racial injustice.

King's message was about love and brotherhood. He worked for change through nonviolent protests. Yet he was often a victim of violence because of his beliefs. During the bus boycott, terrorists bombed his home. He had been kicked, shoved, and even stabbed.

When Alice saw Dr. King on television, he was being arrested because of a protest march he had led in Alabama. She watched him being pushed into the police van. In the background demonstrators were singing "We Shall Overcome." It was a song that became associated with the Civil Rights Movement. Even under those circumstances, Alice knew that King was someone in whom she could believe. She was filled with hope for the future.[2]

Through these years, Alice's mother realized that her daughter was special. Even when Alice was the only daughter living at home, her mother did not ask her to help with chores around the house. She seemed to recognize that Alice needed a lot of time to think and read. She wanted her daughter to have that opportunity.

Looking back on those years, Walker said, "I could go into my room and shut the door and lie on the bed and read, knowing I would never be interrupted. No matter what was needed, there was no word about making me leave a book."[3] Alice did help with chores around the house, but it was out of love, not because she was expected to do them.

Minnie Walker also gave Alice three gifts, which became symbolic of her belief in her daughter's abilities. Alice knew her mother had bought all three gifts on layaway "out of less than twenty dollars a week she made as a domestic."[4] That knowledge made the gifts even more precious to Alice.

The first gift was a sewing machine. Mrs. Walker gave it to her teenaged daughter as a birthday present so that she could learn to make her own clothes. She wanted her daughter to be independent and self-sufficient. Alice put the gift to good use, even making her prom dress.

The second gift was a typewriter with a small typing table. The message was clear: Go and write.

Mrs. Walker gave Alice the third gift, a suitcase, when she graduated from high school. "That suitcase gave me permission to travel,"[5] Walker said.

Alice Walker with her mother in 1979. Mrs. Walker is holding a photograph of her and her husband taken in the 1930s. Mrs. Walker had great faith in her daughter's abilities.

Ironically, the accident that had caused her blindness in one eye also helped open the door to her future. Because of her disability, Alice qualified for a scholarship given by the Georgia Department of Rehabilitation to physically challenged students. The award was for free textbooks and half of her college expenses. Because of her high grades, she was offered a scholarship from Spelman College which covered the other half of her expenses. The women in her church also took up a collection. They raised $75 to help send Alice to college.

Alice took a bus to Atlanta, where the college was located. She made the mistake of sitting too close to the front. A white woman complained to the driver. The driver asked Alice to move to the back. Walker later wrote, "But even as I moved, in confusion and anger and tears, I knew he had not seen the last of me."[6]

4

"To Hell With Dying"

One of Alice's first political activities at Spelman was to go to Washington, D.C., to picket the White House in 1962. President John F. Kennedy was threatening to go to war with Cuba over what was called the Cuban Missile Crisis, and many people gathered to protest.

The crisis had actually begun several months earlier when Cuban leaders became convinced that the United States was planning to attack. They turned to what was then known as the Soviet Union for help. The Soviet Union responded by sending missiles and materials to build launch sites.

Kennedy ordered a naval blockade in an attempt to stop the Soviet Union from sending more supplies. For several days the world waited. It seemed that the two nations were on the brink of nuclear war.

Walker did not believe in violence. She joined the protesters in front of the White House as a call for peace. It was the middle of winter and the picketers hunkered down in their heavy jackets, trying to stay warm. Kennedy looked out and saw the demonstrators shivering in the cold. Then he sent them coffee and tea. Walker always remembered that act of kindness from the man whose actions they were there to protest.[1]

The summer after her freshman year at Spelman, Walker got a chance to attend the World Youth Peace Festival in Helsinki, Finland. It was her first trip abroad. Women from Atlanta's African-American churches raised the money to send Walker and another student from Spelman to the conference. Their advisor suggested that they meet with Coretta Scott King before they left. Mrs. King, the wife of Dr. Martin Luther King, Jr., was very active in working for peace.

Walker and her friend were to meet with Mrs. King at her home. The Kings lived in a red-brick house on Sunset Avenue, only a few blocks from where Walker herself lived. Walker described the King's home as "bare-looking" and "modest"—the kind of house other African Americans would live in. It made her happy to know that the man who had come to have such an influence on her life lived like the people he represented.[2]

During the school year, Walker participated in demonstrations held in downtown Atlanta on Saturday

Alice Walker attended Spelman College from 1961 to 1963. In 1987 she returned to the campus to give an address in honor of Founder's Day. She was presented with this sweatshirt.

mornings. They were organized by a group called the Student Nonviolent Coordinating Committee (SNCC).

The summer after her sophomore year, Walker heard King deliver his most famous address. She was working in Boston to earn money for the next year's college expenses. In August she traveled by bus to Washington, D.C., to participate in the March on Washington for Jobs and Freedom. The event was meant to call attention to the high unemployment rate among African Americans. It was also a show of support for a civil rights bill President Kennedy had proposed to Congress.

About two hundred thousand blacks and whites turned out for the march from the Washington Monument to the Lincoln Memorial. Because of the crowd, Walker could not get close to the speakers. In fact, she could not even *see* them! But she could hear their voices. She sat in the distance on the limb of a tree and listened.

The high point of the day was when King delivered his "I Have a Dream" speech. That day, for the first time, Walker heard an African American telling his people to "go back to Mississippi."[3] Until then, African Americans had been urged to leave the South. It was their only opportunity for a better life. That day King encouraged African Americans to work for change wherever they lived, including the South.

After her sophomore year at Spelman, Walker received another scholarship. This one made it possible

Over two hundred thousand people gathered at the Lincoln Memorial where Martin Luther King, Jr., gave his famous "I Have a Dream" speech. Alice Walker was there too and felt the excitement of the crowd.

for her to transfer to Sarah Lawrence College in Bronxville, New York.

At Sarah Lawrence, Walker felt she had more freedom.[4] She also found support for her writing there. On the other hand, she had gone from an all-black school to a college that had only six African-American students. For the first time she was in "an almost totally white society."[5]

In 1964, the summer before her senior year at Sarah Lawrence, Walker received a fellowship to travel to East Africa. There she helped build a school in Kenya. After leaving Africa, she traveled through Europe. She returned from her journey "loaded down with sculptures and orange fabric"[6]—reminders of her summer in Africa.

Her happiness was soon overshadowed when she learned that she was pregnant. She was very sick with her pregnancy. She lay in bed trying to figure out what to do. Some women in her situation put their faith in "maternal instincts." Once their babies were born they thought that their natural mothering abilities would take over and everything would be all right. Walker could not share their optimism. She was not sure she even had maternal instincts.[7]

She could not turn to her parents for help. Her father had made his feelings clear about pregnancy out of wedlock. He could be very harsh with his daughters, especially his middle daughter Ruth. Once he had beaten her, locked her in her room, and told her "never to come home if she found herself pregnant."[8]

Walker later learned why her father acted the way he did. When he was eleven years old, his mother had been murdered on her way home from church by a man she had rejected. Walker said her father "was just crazed by this early pain."[9] Ruth was the daughter who looked most like his mother.

Walker thought about abortion. She knew her mother would not approve.[10] It did not seem to matter. Neither Walker nor her friends knew how to find a doctor who would do the procedure.

Walker then began to plan her suicide.[11] For three nights she slept with a razor under her pillow preparing for her death. Then one of her friends rescued her. She had found a doctor who would perform the abortion.[12]

The week following the abortion, Walker did nothing but write poems. She poured all her thoughts into a little blue notebook, stopping only to eat and sleep. She wrote about Africa and her thoughts on suicide. She wrote love poems and poems about her experiences in the Civil Rights Movement.

Each morning she took the poems she had written the day before and slid them under the door of her mentor and teacher Muriel Rukeyser. Rukeyser was also a poet. Walker did not care what her teacher did with the poems. She only knew that she needed to have someone read them.

Rukeyser gave the poems to her agent, who sent them to an editor at a large New York publishing house. The editor liked the poems and immediately accepted them. Three years later the collection, titled *Once*, was published.

Although the book was written in sadness, Walker called it a "happy" book.[13] It was filled with color, hope, pride, friendship, and love. Walker says that she wrote the African poems first because the images all came back to her one night in a dream.[14] There were poems about the color and beauty of Africa, and poems that showed the pride of the African people.

In a review for *Library Journal*, Estelle Benedict said the poems about Africa "resemble colored slides moving one by one through a projector."[15] Lisel Mueller of *Poetry* called them "pencil sketches."[16]

Walker says that some of the love poems were real, but others were only imagined. In a poem called "Johann" she wrote about love with a young German man. In reality, Walker says that when she traveled through Germany that summer, she "was in a constant state of terror."[17] She would not have even considered the advances of a young German man.

The title poem "Once" was about Walker's experiences during the Civil Rights Movement. "Chic Freedom's Reflection" was also about that time. Walker often participated in civil rights marches. The demonstrators walked side by side, holding one another's hand so they

Alice Walker as a student at Sarah Lawrence College with her teacher and mentor Muriel Rukeyser. Rukeyser played a key role in getting Walker's first book of poetry published.

did not feel so afraid. The woman Walker wrote about in this poem was one of her marching partners. Walker described her as "a beautiful girl who spoke French."[18] In the poem the woman stands on her tiptoes to powder her nose. She uses a policeman's badge as her mirror. The book of poems was an immediate success. It went into a second printing right away.

Rukeyser also played a part in the publication of Walker's first short story, "To Hell with Dying." It is about Mr. Sweet, an old man who is saved from death many times by his neighbor's children.

Each time Mr. Sweet lies dying, a neighbor man brings his children into the room, pushes the doctor out of the way, and says in a very loud voice, "To hell with dying man, these children want Mr. Sweet!"[19] Then the children kiss him and tickle him back to life. The narrator of the story is one of the children.

There was a real Mr. Sweet in Walker's life. He was an older man who played the guitar. Walker remembered him coming to her grandmother's house when she was about eight or nine years old. He would sit in an oak-bottomed chair, playing his guitar that he called a "box."

He was a gambler who drank and liked to "shoot off his gun."[20] But he was always welcome in their kitchen. The children were taught to respect him because he was an artist. Walker says, "He went deep into his own pain and brought out words and music that made us happy, made us feel empathy for anyone in trouble, made us think."[21]

In the story the narrator is called home from college to try and save Mr. Sweet one more time. In real life, Walker learned of her Mr. Sweet's death during the Christmas holidays. She was too poor to go home for his funeral, a distance of about one thousand miles. Instead she spent the break at a friend's house. Tears streamed down her face as she wrote the story on the day her Mr. Sweet was buried.

Muriel Rukeyser sent the story to Langston Hughes. Hughes was one of the first African-American writers to gain a wide readership in America. He liked the story, and published it two years later in a book titled *Best Short Stories by Negro Writers*. In 1988 "To Hell with Dying" was published as a children's picture book.

Walker later got a chance to meet Langston Hughes. As soon as she saw him she knew she had found another Mr. Sweet. He was "aging and battered, full of pain, but writing poetry, and laughing, too, and always making other people feel better."[22]

5

"The Stories Are Knee-Deep"

"The real revolution is always concerned with the least glamorous stuff,"[1] Walker once wrote. The work behind the scenes of the Civil Rights Movement was not what made the evening news. Registering voters or helping people fill out forms to get food stamps were important, but not newsworthy, tasks.

These were the matters Walker turned her attention to after her graduation from Sarah Lawrence College. She spent part of the summer in Liberty County, Georgia, registering voters. Then she moved to New York and got a job with the New York City Welfare Department. She also continued her writing—working during the day and writing at night.

In 1966 she received her first writing grant—money given to writers who show outstanding talent. Grants help writers with their living expenses so that they can concentrate on their writing. Walker had planned to go to Senegal, West Africa, to write, but instead went to Mississippi.

She did not know anyone in Mississippi. In her mind it was a frightening place for an African American to live.[2] Yet that was where she decided to go. She later explained her decision. "That summer marked the beginning of a realization that I could never live happily in Africa—or anywhere else—until I could live freely in Mississippi."[3]

There she met a white law student named Mel Leventhal. He was in Mississippi for the summer, working in the Civil Rights Movement. The two fell in love. That fall he went back to New York for his final year of school, and Walker went with him.

Leventhal was supportive of Walker's writing. He also understood her love of nature and her longing for the country. He set up a writing area for Walker in his apartment. Walker's own apartment was dark, damp, and a haven for roaches. Leventhal's had a large double window with a view of Washington Square. Leventhal brought a table from his mother's home and set it up in front of the window. Walker covered it with a madras bedspread and set a brown earthenware vase on it. They kept the vase filled with flowers—white daisies, colorful tulips, or sometimes, pink peonies. The flowers were an attempt to give her work area the "feel" of the country.

In New York City, Alice Walker decorated her work area with flowers. She wanted the "feel" of the country as she wrote. Here she enjoys the flowers on the Spelman College campus in 1987.

At this table, Walker wrote an essay that won first prize in the annual *American Scholar* magazine essay contest. It was called "The Civil Rights Movement: What Good Was It?"

Some people had complained that the Civil Rights Movement failed because it did not give African Americans what they wanted. In her essay, Walker listed all the good effects that the movement had accomplished. She said it gave them hope for the future, and brought an end to a pattern of African Americans as servants. The movement also gave them heroes such as Dr. Martin Luther King, Jr. Most of all, it gave them each other.

The award-winning article was Walker's first published essay. The $300 prize kept the young couple in spending money for several months.

While in New York, Walker began writing her first novel. However, she soon realized that she needed a quiet place away from the city where she could work. She applied for and received a fellowship from the MacDowell Colony in rural New Hampshire. It allowed her to live at the colony and write full time—without outside distractions.

At MacDowell, the snow piled high outside the window of her cabin. Inside, warm by a fire, Walker wrote. Leventhal drove his little red Volkswagen to visit her on the weekends. He brought her "flowers, grapefruit, and oranges."[4]

Walker stayed at MacDowell about six weeks and finished several chapters of her book. Then she gave up her fellowship and went back to New York to marry Leventhal. They exchanged vows on March 17, 1967.

Leventhal finished law school in the spring. After his graduation, the couple returned to Mississippi. Leventhal worked as a civil rights lawyer. His job was to sue institutions that discriminated because of race. Eventually he became the prosecutor in the Jackson school desegregation cases.

Walker got a job as a consultant in African-American history for a Headstart program called Friends of the Children of Mississippi. She instructed teachers on how to teach African-American history to the children.

Ninety women from around the state attended her workshops. They were from all different backgrounds. Some of them had taught in the Georgia school system, but many of them had been maids or field workers. The average level of education for the group was about fifth grade.

It was hard to know how to teach such a diverse group. Walker decided to have them write their own histories. She felt it was more important to give them a sense of what history is, rather than teach them a lot of facts (although she did that too).[5] The job ended when funding for the program was cut.

It was a difficult time for an interracial couple to live in Mississippi. There had been a state law ordering that they could not live in the same home. This law had been ruled unconstitutional by the U.S. Supreme Court three months before they moved there. Even so, the two were afraid their home would be attacked by people who did not approve of their marriage.[6] They lived with a big dog and a rifle by the door.

Walker also worried about her husband.[7] Not everyone agreed with the work he was trying to do. Some considered him an "outside agitator." His work took him deep into the Mississippi backwoods to visit clients. Walker was afraid that he might not return from one of those trips.[8]

In spite of the racial tension, Walker's writing flourished. She wanted to tell the stories of southern African-American women. She felt that as a group they were doubly oppressed—first, because they were black, and second, because they were women.[9] Mississippi was full of their stories. In a letter to a friend, Walker wrote that she would be staying there for a while because "the stories are knee-deep."[10]

Walker wrote poems, short stories, essays, and continued working on her novel. For a while it seemed as though there was so much to write that she just could not get it all down fast enough.

Then in 1968, Dr. Martin Luther King, Jr., was assassinated. In an article for *Redbook* magazine Walker wrote: "It was as if the last light in my world had gone out."[11]

Walker and her husband made the trip to Atlanta for King's funeral. They joined 200,000 other Americans for the four-mile walk through the hot city streets. They marched behind a mule-drawn farm wagon that carried King's casket. The wagon was a symbol of the poverty he had tried to end.

Walker was pregnant at the time. A week later she had a miscarriage. She lay in bed not caring if she lived or died.[12] Then one day she saw Mrs. King on television. Mrs. King was in New York delivering a speech. It was only three weeks after her husband's death, but Mrs. King said that she thought he would want her to be there. She said it was important that she continued with his work.

Seeing Coretta Scott King's courage gave Walker strength. She began to think her own grief was self-pity.[13] It was time to get back to work.

Walker turned to her writing, as she often did when she wanted to pull herself out of depression. She has said many times that writing has saved her life. In an interview with Claudia Dreifus for *The Progressive*, Walker explained how the process works:

> It's like in Native-American cultures, when you feel sick at heart, sick in soul, you do sand paintings. Or you make a basket. The thing is that you are focused on creating something. And while you're doing that, there's a kind of spiritual alchemy that happens and you turn that bad feeling into something that becomes a golden light.[14]

Walker says that writing also helps her explore her feelings. "After it is written down, I can look at it in a more objective way and see what is happening within myself."[15]

Walker wrote and taught classes at Jackson State University. She also learned that she was pregnant again. In 1969 she finished her first novel three days before the birth of her daughter Rebecca.

In 1970, Walker was appointed writer-in-residence at Tougaloo College in Tougaloo, Mississippi. That year her first novel, *The Third Life of Grange Copeland* was published. That novel exposed violence against women at a time when other people had not even begun to talk about the issue. The book is about three stages in Grange Copeland's life.

In his first life, Grange is a sharecropper. He has given in to the defeat caused by poverty. His life has fallen into a pattern. All week he works long hours for the white landowner whom he hates. On Saturday he goes into town for groceries and comes home roaring drunk. He threatens his wife and frightens their only child Brownfield. On Sunday they go to church as a family. By supper time he is fighting with his wife. The pattern repeats with the start of a new week.

His wife decides to get back at him by having an affair with the landowner. She has another son as a result of that liaison. Grange abandons his family, knowing that if he stays he will kill his wife. When his wife

A family photo taken in 1970 shows Mel Leventhal, Alice
Walker, and their daughter Rebecca.

realizes that he is not coming back, she kills herself and her illegitimate son. Brownfield is left on his own.

The second stage of Grange's life takes place in the North where he beats up as many white men as he can. Eventually he begins to see that he cannot blame white men for all his problems. That kind of thinking gives them too much power. Gradually he begins to discover his own self-worth.

Here the book also takes up Brownfield's life and his fight for survival on his own. He starts out determined to have a life very different from his father's. He marries an intelligent, well-educated, and tender woman, but he is unable to really love her. He begins a cruel campaign to destroy her—to bring her down to his level. He forces her into the life of a sharecropper and the poverty that comes with it. This is in spite of the fact that she is capable of providing a much better life for them in town. He beats her and finally, when she has no hope left, he kills her.

By this time, Grange has come back to town a changed man. While Brownfield is in prison, Grange takes in his youngest granddaughter Ruth. With her, he is able to be the father he was not capable of being with his son. When Brownfield is released from prison he tries to get Ruth back. To prevent that from happening, Grange kills his son and sacrifices his own life.

Josephine Hendin of *Saturday Review* called the book "a powerful story."[16] Robert Coles from *The New*

Yorker wrote, "What goes on between that daughter, that growing child, and her grandfather is told with particular grace; it is as if one were reading a long and touching poem."[17]

Walker was also criticized, partially, because of her portrayal of men. It was a criticism that she would hear often throughout her career. The complaint was that the young men in her books were angry unlikable people. It seemed that she only wrote sympathetically about older men.

In an interview with David Bradley for *The New York Times Magazine*, Walker told how her personal life had influenced her perception of older men. She recounted:

> I knew both my grandfathers, and they were just doting, indulgent, sweet old men. . . . However, as young men, middle-aged men, they were . . . brutal. One grandfather knocked my grandmother out of a window. He beat one of his children so severely that the child had epilepsy. Just a horrible, horrible man. But when I knew him, he was a sensitive, wonderful man.[18]

Others were critical because of the violence in the book. The scene where Brownfield murdered his wife was especially shocking. But Walker wrote about subjects she wanted others to know about. That scene was based on a true incident from her own past.

When she was thirteen, her sister worked in a local funeral home. There Alice saw the body of the woman she wrote about in her book. Her husband had shot her in the face. She was lying there with one shoe hanging from the toe of her foot. The sole of the shoe had a hole in it, and the woman had covered it with newspaper.

"Maybe there are writers who can see this and write nothing, but I'm not one of them," Walker told an interviewer. "Something needs to be said about this totally wanton, cruel behavior that caused this woman's death. I was happy to be able to say something."[19]

6

Zora

Walker never got to study the works of other African-American women authors when she was in college. They were not mentioned in any of her classes. She felt this omission left a hole in her education.[1]

She wanted a sense of history—knowledge of what had been written by others before her. As a writer, she was looking for role models. But it was by accident that she discovered the author who would have the greatest influence on her work.

It began with a story that her mother used to tell about the Great Depression of the 1930s. Food was hard to get then—especially flour. People in need were given vouchers that entitled them to free flour from the government. The flour was distributed by the Red Cross.

Minnie Walker had vouchers, and was going into town for the flour. She wore a dress that she had pulled out of a box of clothes she had just received. The clothes were hand-me-downs from one of Walker's aunts who lived in the North.

At the distribution center she gave the vouchers to the white woman behind the counter. The woman looked Mrs. Walker up and down. Then she told Mrs. Walker that she was dressed too nicely to be there. The woman said that Mrs. Walker should not be begging for what she obviously did not need.

Mrs. Walker fought back tears. She tried to explain that the clothes were given to her. The woman would not listen. She had already moved on to the next person in line.

Walker heard her mother tell this particular story many times. To Walker, it seemed that her mother held her head a little higher each time she told the story.[2]

The woman who had turned away Mrs. Walker that day became very crippled as she grew older. She had to use two canes to walk. Some people might say that this turn of events was God's work. Others would call it justice. But the writer in Walker asked "What if?" What if "after the crippled old lady died, it was discovered that someone . . . had voodooed her?"[3]

The idea fascinated Walker. But first she needed to find out as much as she could about the practice of

54

voodoo among rural southern African Americans in the 1930s.

The research was difficult. All the books she found on the subject were written by white authors. Walker felt that these writers did not respect the African-American culture. She was not sure that she could trust their reliability.[4] Then Walker found a footnote referring to a book called *Mules and Men*. The author was Zora Neale Hurston.

Hurston was a collector of African-American folklore. She wrote down stories that were gradually disappearing from her culture. They were tales that African Americans had forgotten or had put aside because they were ashamed of them. They thought the stories made them appear ignorant or peculiar to white people. Hurston did not share their embarrassment. She saw the stories as a part of their history.

Walker combined the information on voodoo that she learned from Hurston's book with her mother's story of the Depression. The result was a short story titled "The Revenge of Hannah Kemhuff."

Hannah Kemhuff was the young mother of four children. She worked as a cook at a saw mill. Her husband had been unemployed for some time. When the mill closed down, her family had no money for food. They were forced to use food stamps provided by the government.

The whole family made the trip into town for the food. However, Hannah was a proud woman so she first dressed them in clothes sent from her sister in the North. At the distribution center, the scene was very similar to what happened to Walker's mother. Hannah noticed that the other people in line were all dressed in tattered dirty clothes. She knew that they had better clothing at home.

The young white girl behind the counter saw Hannah's family in their fine clothes. She told them they did not need the food. She gave their share to the old gambler behind them in line. He got double the amount of food he had coming.

Hannah's husband had been unfaithful to his wife. His lover was also at the distribution center that day. He helped her carry her food out to the car she was driving. Hannah never saw him again. She was left alone with her hungry children. One by one her children starved to death.

Years later Hannah contracted a conjurer named Tante Rosie. She wanted to get revenge on Mrs. Holley, the woman who as a young girl had turned her away that day. The narrator of the story was an apprentice to Tante Rosie. The apprentice and the conjurer did succeed in getting revenge for Hannah. They used Mrs. Holley's own fear and guilt as their tools.

Hurston had written four novels, two books of folklore, and her autobiography. Walker read them all.

Alice Walker admired Zora Neale Hurston's talent and courage. This photo of Hurston was taken by photographer Carl Van Vechten.

She especially liked a love story titled *Their Eyes Were Watching God*.

Because Walker enjoyed Hurston's books so much, she wanted to know what others said about her. She looked up reviews of Hurston's work. She found that critics had cruelly attacked Hurston. Much of their criticism was about her lifestyle instead of what she had written.

They said she received grants and fellowships too easily from white people. They thought she had too many lovers. They even found fault with her dress, since she liked to wear scarves wrapped around her head the way black women in Africa and Haiti did.

Walker read the attacks on Hurston and became "paralyzed with confusion and fear."[5] Would she also be criticized for expressing her opinions? Walker tried to figure out why critics disliked Hurston so much. She thought it may have been because Hurston's behavior could be so outrageous. Walker told about a time when Hurston's play, *Color Struck!*, won second place in a literary contest. "Hurston walked into a room full of her competitors, flung her scarf dramatically over her shoulder, and yelled 'COLOR . . R . R STRUCK . . K . K!' at the top of her voice."[6] Some people were put off by Hurston's actions. Walker said that apparently these people expected Hurston to be humble about winning only second place.

According to Walker, Hurston always said exactly what was on her mind. This was another trait that upset her critics. At that time neither women nor African Americans were supposed to be so outspoken.

Walker decided that, like Hurston, she would not be silenced by critics. She would continue to write what she thought needed to be said.

Eventually the depression that had haunted Walker off and on for much of her life began to return.[7] Part of the reason was because it was hard to mix motherhood with writing. She no longer had large blocks of uninterrupted time for thinking and writing. She had lost the easy mobility she had enjoyed in the past. Research trips now had to be planned around her child's schedule.

Another cause for her depression came from being a pacifist during a violent time. African Americans had been beaten, arrested, and even killed as they fought for equal rights. Walker worked for change too through her writing, but was it enough? To her, it seemed as though others were doing so much more.[8]

Walker knew that she needed a rest from Mississippi. In 1972, she took her young daughter and moved to Massachusetts. Her husband stayed in Mississippi to continue his work. In Cambridge, Walker taught a course on African-American women writers at Wellesley College. Then she taught this course at the University of Massachusetts in Boston. This was the only class of its kind at that time. One of the novels Walker had her students study was Hurston's *Their Eyes Were Watching God.*

In August 1973, Walker made a very personal journey. Even though Hurston was a talented writer, she had died in poverty. She was buried in an unmarked grave somewhere in Florida. Walker wanted to put a marker on her grave.

It took some detective work, but Walker finally learned that Hurston was buried in a cemetery called the Garden of Heavenly Rest in Fort Pierce, Florida. Unfortunately the cemetery was now overrun with weeds. Walker knew there were probably snakes too. She tried not to think about the snakes as she hiked up her long skirt and tromped through the weeds. Walker found the gravesite and then went into town and bought a headstone. She had it engraved with the words:

Zora Neale Hurston
"A Genius of the South"[9]

After that trip, Walker wrote an essay called "In Search of Zora Neale Hurston." It was published in the March 1975 issue of *Ms.* magazine. It told about finding Hurston's gravesite and placing a tombstone there. The essay and Walker's teaching began a renewed interest in Hurston's writing.

Walker also edited a collection of Hurston's work, which was published in 1979. The long title came from

In 1972, Alice Walker taught a class on African-American women writers at Wellesley College. It was the only class of its kind at the time.

a letter written by Hurston to photographer Carl Van Vechten on December 10, 1934. The letter was to thank him for a series of photographs he had taken of her. After seeing the photos she wrote: "I love myself when I am laughing. And then again when I am looking mean and impressive."[10] Her words became the title of Walker's book.

7

"Revolutionary Petunias"

When Walker was a child, there was a lavender petunia that bloomed in her family's yard year after year. Her mother had found it and brought it home long before Walker was even born.

Minnie Walker and her husband had been in their wagon heading home one day. As they rode past a deserted house, she saw a lone petunia blooming among the weeds. "Stop! Let me go and get that petunia bush,"[1] she called to her husband.

She took it home and planted it in their yard. Every spring the petunia blossomed. In the winter it lay dormant. Each time they moved, she dug up the flower and took it with the family. It thrived wherever she planted it. Thirty-seven years later, she gave her daughter Alice a piece of that same petunia bush.

When Walker was writing her second book of poetry, she thought about that flower. It was such a contrast to today's petunias, which die in the fall and have to be replanted each spring. She called the book *Revolutionary Petunias and Other Poems.* In an introduction to the book Walker wrote: "These poems are about . . . (and for) those few embattled souls who remain painfully committed to beauty and to love even while facing the firing squad."[2]

Sammy Lou of the title poem, "Revolutionary Petunias," is that kind of person. She is a farmer's wife and a religious woman. She certainly does not believe in taking another person's life. Yet she does kill a man—the man who murdered her husband. As she goes to the electric chair her only concern is her flowers. She calls to her children, telling them to remember to water her "purple petunias."

Other poems in the book are about the people Walker knew. In "Uncles" she writes about her uncles who lived in the North. "Burial" describes her grandfather at her grandmother's funeral. It also mentions her first-grade teacher, Miss Reynolds.

"For My Sister Molly Who in the Fifties" is about Walker's sister who went away to college. Walker loved having her sister home for vacations. She cooked, cleaned, and answered the younger children's questions.

She also read to them and taught them African songs. However, her sister gradually pulled away from her family. Walker later realized that it was because she was ashamed of them.

Walker started out to write an angry poem. It did not turn out that way, though. In the process of writing the poem, Walker began to understand how her sister felt. She knew that her sister was seeing her family through her college friends' eyes. To them, the Walkers were poor farmers. They did not have a nice home or stylish clothes. They did not talk the way her sister's friends thought they should. Walker worked on the poem, off and on, for five years, writing over fifty drafts. She gave the first draft to her sister.

Revolutionary Petunias and Other Poems won the Lillian Smith award. This is an honor given to writers who contribute to the understanding of the South. It was one of two books Walker had published during 1973. The other was her first collection of short stories called *In Love and Trouble: Stories of Black Women.*

Walker wrote the stories in this collection between 1967 and 1973. This included the time she spent in New York City working for the Welfare Department and her years in Mississippi. Each of the stories is about an episode in the life of an African-American woman. "The Revenge of Hannah Kemhuff" and "To Hell with Dying" are part of the collection.

In a story titled "The Welcome Table," an elderly African-American woman is physically removed from an all-white church. Outside she sees a vision of Jesus coming up the road towards her. She walks with him—"high-stepping down the highway"[3]—until she dies from exhaustion.

The idea for the story came from Walker's days at Spelman College. She remembered walking with a friend one day. They came to a church and decided to go in. As they started up the stairs, white men carrying ax handles appeared and turned them away.

"Roselilly" is about an unwed mother of four who is marrying a Muslim from the North. During the wedding, her thoughts are interweaved with the words of the marriage ceremony. When she hears the words "to join this man and this woman," she is thinking of "ropes, chains, handcuffs, his religion."[4] Her Muslim husband offers her respectability and a better life for her children. In return, she is giving up her freedom.

"The Flowers" is about ten-year-old Myop who is exploring the woods behind her home. Her arms are filled with flowers that she has picked. Suddenly she comes upon the skeleton of a man who has been lynched. She sees the noose: "Frayed, rotted, bleached, and frazzled—barely there—but spinning restlessly in the breeze."[5] She lays down her flowers.

Mel Watkins of *The New York Times Book Review* called *In Love and Trouble* an "impressive collection." He said that Walker was "a skillful recorder of the Southern character."[6]

Barbara Smith reviewed the book for *Ms.* magazine. She said her first reaction was to question the amount of pain these women suffered. Then she went on to say, "I soon realized, however, that the reason these stories saddened me so much was because of their truthfulness. For every one of Walker's fictional women I knew or had heard of a real woman whose fate was all too similar."[7]

In Love and Trouble won the Richard and Hinda Rosenthal Award. This award, from the American Institute of Arts and Letters, is given annually.

In 1974 Walker, her husband, and her daughter moved back to New York. Walker got a job as a contributing editor for *Ms.* magazine, working three days a week. The rest of the time Walker wrote. That year her children's biography *Langston Hughes: American Poet* was published.

Her second novel *Meridian* came out in 1976. It was the first book written about the role women played in the Civil Rights Movement.

The opening scene takes place in a southern town called Chicokema. Truman Held is there to see his friend Meridian Hill. The book is what Walker calls a "crazy-quilt story."[8] It is not written in chronological order. Instead it goes back in time showing key scenes from the lives of the characters.

There are scenes from Meridian's childhood. Meridian thinks her mother should not have had children. Mrs. Hill makes sure that her children are always clean and that their clothes are always spotless, but she does not love them.

Meridian tries to win her mother's approval, but fails. She is haunted by the memory of the day that she finally realized she would never have her mother's love. She was thirteen years old, sitting next to her mother in church. It was the part of the service where believers went up to the front of the church to proclaim Jesus as their personal saviour. Meridian's mother urged her daughter to join them. Meridian could not; she knew she did not believe in that way. Meridian could tell by the look on her mother's face that she had lost her mother's love forever.

Meridian is a good student, but then she gets pregnant. She marries the father of her child and drops out of school. It seemed the only choice for women at that time. Her husband continues his education and works at a restaurant. But he is unfaithful to his wife, and Meridian feels trapped at home with her son.

Meridian meets Truman Held, an African-American college student who is active in the Civil Rights Movement. Through him, Meridian also gets involved in the struggle for equal rights. Gradually she begins to realize that she has choices. She does not have to live the life of sacrifice her mother chose. She is offered a scholarship to go to an all-black women's college in Atlanta. She gives her son to relatives, and sets out on her own.

Meridian is in love with Truman, but he rejects her for white women. He marries Lynne Rabinowitz, a Jewish woman who has come south in support of the Civil Rights Movement. It is a difficult life for Lynne. She is not accepted in the African-American community. Because of her marriage to an African-American man, she cannot go back to her family. Eventually, Truman and Lynne get a divorce.

Truman comes back to Meridian, but she is no longer interested in him. She is committed to improving life for African Americans in the South. Truman, on the other hand, says the Civil Rights Movement is over. People, including him, are not interested in that struggle anymore. He does not understand her dedication.

Throughout the book, Meridian searches for her own identity. She has failed in her mother's eyes because she has rejected her mother's religion and has been unsuccessful as a wife and mother. She believes that she has even failed as a revolutionary. She was asked to leave a radical group in New York because she refused to say that she would kill for the revolution. She was willing to die for the revolution, but was not sure that she could kill for it.

There are many similarities between Meridian and Walker. Like Walker, Meridian gets a scholarship to attend an all-black women's college in Atlanta. There she is active in the Civil Rights Movement and has an abortion. Later, Meridian attends a college in the North. Also, like Walker, she struggles with being a pacifist in a violent world.

There are also differences between the two. Meridian is forced into marriage and has an unwanted child. Also, Meridian and her mother do not enjoy the loving relationship that Walker and her mother shared.

However, the similarities have made some people wonder if the book is autobiographical. Walker says that the character Meridian is actually a composite of several people.[9] She has also said that there is a part of her in all of her characters. "I'm everywhere and I'm everybody," she once told an interviewer. "That's true in all my books."[10]

Reviewers had good things to say about the book. *Liberty Journal* hailed it as "a tight fascinating novel."[11] *The Progressive* declared that *Meridian* was "beautifully written," and that it "helps us to keep alive memories of that dramatic period."[12] In a review for *Commonweal,* Gordon Burnside called *Meridian* "a failure as a novel." On the other hand, he said it was "an extremely interesting historical document."[13]

The same year that *Meridian* was published, Walker and Mel Leventhal were divorced. Walker has never publicly discussed the divorce. She and Leventhal have, however, remained friends and shared custody of their daughter.

Walker says that the poems in her third book of poetry, *Good Night, Willie Lee, I'll See You in the Morning,* were written during a very painful time in her life. "I was shattered by the assassination of so many people I loved during the sixties,"[14] she wrote. She was also affected by the death of her father in 1973 and her divorce.

The title poem recalls her mother's parting words to her husband at his funeral. "Good night, Willie Lee, I'll see you in the morning,"[15] she said.

Walker regrets that she was not closer to her father when he was living.[16] She had loved him as a small child. Later she began to blame him for her family's poverty. At seventeen she headed for college, eager to be leaving behind "the only world he would ever know."[17] She remembered him standing outside the bus that day. He held his hat—"an old gray fedora"[18]—in his hands. Walker had tears in her eyes as the bus carried her farther away from him physically and in spirit.

Walker does feel that she has made peace with her father since his death. She believes that they both now understand that their relationship "was a casualty of exhaustion and circumstances."[19] He was worn out from working hard all his life for very little money. She was determined to put that kind of life behind her.

Walker sent the poems for her third book of poetry to her publisher. Then she began work on another novel.

8

The Color Purple

On the last page of *The Color Purple*, Alice Walker wrote: "I thank everybody in this book for coming. A.W., author and medium." In calling herself a medium, Walker meant that she was acting as an interpreter. She wrote down what her characters communicated to her. This inscription describes her writing style.

In an interview with Gregory Jaynes for *Life* magazine, Walker talked about her writing process. She said that she "moons around" a lot. As she goes about her daily activities, she is not really aware of what is going on around her. Instead, she is thinking about her characters, giving them a chance to develop in her mind. She dreams about them, meditates, and then waits for them to "speak" to her.

The characters from her third novel *The Color Purple* were very particular about when and where they would speak to her. Walker got the idea for the novel when she was hiking with her sister Ruth. They talked about a lover's triangle that they both knew about. Ruth said, "And you know, one day The Wife asked The Other Woman for a pair of her drawers."[1] Walker had been wanting to write an historical novel about "two women who felt married to the same man."[2] Her sister's remark was just what she needed to get the story going. Over the next few months the novel began to take shape in Walker's mind.

At the same time, Walker was looking for a new place to live. She bought a house in the Park Slope section of Brooklyn, New York. She planted a tree in the front yard and another in the back. They were only symbols of the country, but Walker hoped that she had created a spot where she could write her story.

Three months later she realized that she had made a mistake. She needed silence to let her characters develop in her imagination. "If you're silent for a long time, people just arrive in your mind," she says.[3] However, New York was not quiet, but noisy and busy. Her characters did not come to her there. In 1978, Walker sold her house and moved to California.

It was her daughter's year to spend with her father, so Walker traveled alone. She found an apartment in San Francisco. A few months later, *Good Night, Willie Lee, I'll See You in the Morning* was published.

In San Francisco Walker renewed her friendship with Robert Allen. They had first met in 1962 when she was a student at Spelman College and he attended nearby Morehouse College. They went their separate ways then. But now they were both living in San Francisco. Allen was also a writer and he was editor of a magazine called *The Black Scholar.*

Walker loved San Francisco, but her characters did not feel at home there either. There were too many people and too many cars, buses, and buildings. Walker knew then that her characters were country people.[4]

Walker and Allen began spending their weekends exploring the state, looking for a country home to rent. They finally found one in northern California. To Walker, the area looked a lot like Georgia.

Her characters liked it too, but they still were not satisfied. Walker had continued working for *Ms.* magazine as a "long-distance editor."[5] She also traveled across the country giving lectures and poetry readings. These activities supplemented her writing income, which could sometimes be unpredictable. But her characters wanted her complete attention. In an interview with her friend Gloria Steinem, Walker said: "The people in the book were willing to visit me but only after I stopped interrupting with poetry readings and lectures and getting on some plane."[6]

Walker cleared her calendar. She turned down requests for speaking engagements. Then she explained her situation to the editors at *Ms.* magazine. They were very supportive. In fact, they continued paying Walker her monthly retainer.

Walker also sold her second collection of short stories called *You Can't Keep a Good Woman Down*. The book was not actually published until 1981. However, with the advance she received for that book and the income from *Ms.* magazine, Walker figured she might have enough to live on for a year. She would have to be careful with her spending though.

Walker bought fabric for a quilt and retreated to her home in the country. She worked on her quilt, took long walks, and enjoyed the quiet. Weeks passed. Walker's quilt got bigger and her characters began telling her their stories. Then summer was over.

Walker's daughter Rebecca would be arriving to spend the next two years with her. Walker wondered how her daughter's arrival would affect the relationship she had developed with her characters.[7] Would they like Rebecca? Or would they suddenly be silent with her there?

Walker soon had her answer. It came one afternoon when Rebecca arrived home from her elementary school looking like she had been in a fight. She said, "Don't worry, Mom. You should see the other guy!"[8] Walker's characters liked Rebecca's "spirit."

Walker had expected to take five years to write the book. She thought she could go back to teaching and

A portrait of Alice Walker taken at the time she was writing *The Color Purple*.

speaking when she needed money. As it turned out, she finished the book a year after she started the actual writing. It was the day her daughter was to leave for summer camp.

Walker felt as though everyone was leaving her—her daughter and the fictional characters who had been living in her head for so long.[9] All that she had left was her quilt and her friend Robert Allen. She fell into his arms and cried.

Walker had earned a reputation as a writer who spoke against injustice without holding back. *The Color Purple* is no exception. The first page shows Celie as a fourteen-year-old girl who is raped by her mother's husband. He warns her that she is not to speak about it to anyone except God. Because she has no one else to talk to, Celie begins writing letters to God.

Celie is forced to quit school because she is pregnant. She has two children from rape, and they are both taken from her at birth. She is then married off to a widower who treats her as a servant—someone to cook, clean, and take care of his children. He physically and verbally abuses her. His real love is a blues singer named Shug Avery.

In the first few pages of the book, Celie has to bear more than most people do in a lifetime. Her life seems completely hopeless. That is when the story of Celie's triumph begins. Little by little, she begins to change her life, becoming more confident and self-sufficient.

The characters in the book are modeled after people Walker knew. Celie is based on Walker's great-great-grandmother. She was a slave who was raped by her master and had his child when she was eleven years old.

Shug Avery is a composite of Zora Neale Hurston and Walker's aunts who lived in the North. Her aunts worked as domestics, but Walker says that they always looked as though they should have had someone to clean *their* houses. "They had wonderful nails, and were all beautifully dressed—just fantastically vibrant women with great perfumes," Walker says. "It still astonishes me that my aunts worked every day for other people and yet retained such a magical life of their own."[10]

Celie writes her letters in what Walker calls "black folk English."[11] Walker rejects the term *dialect*, calling it "racist." She says that when authors write in dialect, they use a lot of apostrophes and contractions. She believes it is their way of showing the reader that they really do know the correct spelling of the words.[12]

There is nothing hidden in Celie's language. She says exactly what is on her mind. The reader shares her pain when Celie writes about the day her father forced her to drop out of school:

> The first time I got big Pa took me out of school. He never care that I love it. Nettie stood there at the gate holding tight to my hand. I was all dress for first day. You too dumb to keep going to school, Pa say. Nettie the clever one in this bunch.[13]

Later, her ability to see humor in a situation comes through when she describes the day "Mister" arrives with the ailing Shug Avery. "Mister" and his son Harpo are helping Shug out of a wagon. Celie writes:

> She looks so stylish it like the trees all round the house draw themself up tall for a better look. Now I see she stumble, tween the two men. She don't seem that well acquainted with her feets.[14]

Celie writes the way Walker's parents and grandparents spoke. It is a language Walker loves because it is brief and to the point. "People said what they had to say," Walker says. "They did not beat around the bush."[15] Walker wanted to preserve the language of her ancestors, especially for her daughter.

Reviewers praised Walker for telling the story in Celie's voice. Mel Watkins of *The New York Times Book Review* called the novel "convincing because of the authenticity of its folk voice."[16]

In an article for *Ms.* magazine, Gloria Steinem said, "Celie just writes her heart out, putting words down the way they feel and sound. Pretty soon you can't imagine why anyone would bother to write any other way."[17]

Perhaps it is Celie herself who best explains the importance of using her own language. In the book Celie meets a woman named Darlene who tells her that Shug would like her more if she talked better. She tries to teach

Celie the "right" way to speak by correcting her whenever she says something wrong. Celie writes:

> Every time I say something the way I say it, she correct me until I say it some other way. Pretty soon it feel like I can't think. My mind run up on a thought, git confuse, run back and sort of lay down.[18]

The Color Purple raised Walker's popularity as a writer to a new level. People were captivated by Celie's story. The book became required reading in many classrooms. It was used not only in literature classes, but also in sociology and history classes. At Kenyon College in Ohio, the book was studied in three different courses in three different departments in one semester.

After writing *The Color Purple* in 1982, Walker went back to teaching. She became a Distinguished Writer in the Department of African-American Studies at the University of California, Berkeley that spring, and taught creative writing at Brandeis University that fall. She also began traveling again for poetry readings and lectures. But success soon changed her life.

As *The Color Purple* topped best-seller lists, Walker received more requests for personal appearances and interviews. People were eager to know more about her. The demands on Walker's time left her feeling tired and longing for the quiet she needed for her writing. She also regretted that she did not have more time to devote to issues she believed in. "I have felt often that I have almost lost a couple of years," Walker told a reporter. ". . . part of my energy that would have gone into being more active, although I have been fairly active, I've had to spend responding to the success."[19]

She was able to answer some of her fans' questions by putting together a collection of her essays, speeches, and reviews. They were pieces she had written over a period of seventeen years. Many of them had already been published in other sources. The book, called *In Search of Our Mothers' Gardens: Womanist Prose*, was published in 1983. It served as her autobiography.

In the book, Walker wrote about her childhood— growing up as a sharecropper's daughter, the accident that left her blind in one eye, and her mother's flowers. There were essays about her college years, the Civil Rights Movement, and Dr. Martin Luther King, Jr. She told about writing *The Color Purple* and how Zora Neale Hurston had influenced her writing.

Walker fought to keep the word *womanist* in the title. A *womanist* she says is "a black feminist."[20] As a poet, Walker tries to use as few words as possible. She did not want to add the word *black* to describe something. Instead, she chose a word from her own culture that said exactly what she wanted to say.

In the African-American culture, if a girl is acting "womanish" she is being assertive. "She is being who she is,"[21] Walker explains. It describes someone, like Walker, who speaks out or says what is on her mind.

A 1984 photo of Alice Walker and her daughter Rebecca. Walker dedicated her first book of essays called *In Search of Our Mothers' Gardens: Womanist Prose* to Rebecca.

Walker was not the first "womanist" in her family. There were many strong independent women among her ancestors. She had always admired her great-great-grandmother who had walked from Virginia to Georgia with a baby on each hip in order to escape oppression.

Walker also admired her mother's strength and determination. "I grew up thinking that there was nothing, literally nothing, my mother couldn't do once she set her mind to it,"[22] she told an interviewer. Walker says she was "delighted" when the women's movement was renewed. "I felt they were trying to go where my mother was and where I always assumed I would go."[23]

9

Changes

Walker was able to write her fourth book of poetry only after she moved to California. She says that in New York her "spirit" was "cramped."[1] California gave her the freedom she needed to think about two prominent themes in the book. "I could, for the first time, admit and express my grief over the ongoing assassination of the earth,"[2] she wrote. She could also explore her heritage.

The book called *Horses Make a Landscape Look More Beautiful* was published in 1984. The title was a quote from a Native American holy person named Lame Deer. He said that white people gave Native Americans horses. Unfortunately they also gave them whiskey. Lame Deer felt that Native Americans could almost forgive white people for giving them whiskey because of the horses. "Horses make a landscape look more beautiful,"[3] he explained.

The book reflected changes in Walker's writing. Her main focus had always been African-American women—their oppressions and their triumphs. That focus would not change. However, she was also beginning to reach out to other groups of people and to speak on other issues. One of those issues was the environment.

In a poem called "Who?," Walker wonders who or what is safe from the destructiveness of the Wasichus. *Wasichus* is a Sioux word meaning "he who takes the fat."[4] It was the Sioux word for white people. Walker said the Wasichus had invaded people, trees, water, rocks, and the air. She thought surely the moon was safe, but concluded it was not. In this case, the term *Wasichus* could be interpreted as anyone who does not protect the environment.

In "The Diamonds on Liz's Bosom," Walker criticized the mining of diamonds and other precious stones. Although she is concerned about the environment, in this poem she was also angry about the danger to the Africans who are forced to work in the mines just to adorn the rich.

In a poem titled "We Alone," she wrote about what she sees as an obsession with gold. She urged jewelry wearers to replace their gold with jewelry made from "feathers, shells and sea-shaped stones,"[5] which are more beautiful. In a long poem titled "These Days" she asks that the world be saved for the people we care about.

Another prominent theme in *Horses Make a Landscape Look More Beautiful* is Walker's search to know her ancestors. Walker says that people must be themselves even if others do not accept them. Denying any part of ourselves can cause suffering.[6] For that reason, Walker spent time learning more about her ancestors, trying to acknowledge every part of her heritage—good and bad.

The book is dedicated to two of Walker's ancestors. One is Tallulah, her great-grandmother on her mother's side who was part Cherokee. The other is her great-great-grandfather on her father's side. The only information Walker knew about him was that he had raped his slave who was Walker's great-great-grandmother.

Walker easily got in touch with her Native American ancestry. According to her, African Americans and Native Americans had some experiences in common. She said that they shared a history of poverty and they had both suffered at the hand of the Wasichus.

Walker had more difficulty acknowledging her white ancestor, since the only information she knew about him was his act of violence against her great-great-grandmother. A poem titled "Family Of" is about her white ancestor. "The Thing Itself" recounts the actual rape.

In the book, Walker also speaks about violence and hunger. Other poems are about her Mississippi days, writing poetry, and family and friends.

In the same year that *Horses* was published, Walker and Robert Allen began their own publishing company called Wild Trees Press. They planned to remain small, publishing only a few books a year. "Manuscripts we love and can't bear to not have available,"[7] Walker told *Ms.* magazine.

Walker's own books were published by a major publishing company. This company had the finances to print and distribute large quantities of her books. A small company such as Wild Trees Press could not compete on that level. However, Walker knew there were other writers who deserved attention but were not being published. Wild Trees Press gave these writers a start.

Most of the books the small company published were by first-time authors. All of the published books showed political awareness. "I don't think we would publish a book, no matter how beautifully written, about people who never change politically. . . . That wouldn't be worth the paper,"[8] Walker said.

In the meantime, film director Steven Spielberg had shown an interest in making *The Color Purple* into a movie. Film producers Peter Guber and Jon Peters made an offer to Walker for the film rights to the book. Walker did not know if she wanted to accept it. Guber and Peters had produced very successful films such as

Flashdance and *Missing*, but they were strangers to her. Because of her writing, Walker lived a reclusive life. She rarely watched television and she seldom went to movies.

Guber and Peters told her that Steven Spielberg would be directing the movie. He had done several well-known films—*Close Encounters of the Third Kind*, *E.T.*, and *Raiders of the Lost Ark*. But Walker had not heard of him either.

She became more interested in the idea of making a movie of her book when she found out that she would be working closely with Quincy Jones. Jones had written musical scores for more than thirty films and also for the *Roots* television miniseries. He had produced Michael Jackson's *Thriller* album and the *We Are the World* album. Walker knew Jones's work and believed that she could trust him.[9] The *We Are the World* project featured forty-five rock and pop artists. The proceeds from the album went to African famine relief. It was an example of one of the reasons Walker liked Jones. "He has a social conscience,"[10] she said.

Jones brought Steven Spielberg to meet Walker. They arrived in Spielberg's limousine, which was so big that it did not fit into her driveway. Walker listened as Spielberg described the movie he wanted to make. He had a "vision" of the film. Walker liked his ideas.

By that time, Walker had found out some information about Spielberg. She knew about the other films he had made. She joked with her daughter Rebecca, saying, "Well, maybe if he can do Martians, he can do us."[11]

In the end, the reason Walker finally agreed to make the movie was because she knew that she would be able to reach a larger audience. The book has a message, which is that anyone can triumph. "There are so many people like Celie who make it, who come out of nothing," Walker said.[12] It was a message she wanted others to hear. She hoped that some of the people who did not read the book, would see the movie.

Walker was able to get some of her own terms written into the movie contract. One of her requirements was that half of the offscreen crew would be "women or blacks or Third World people."[13] Third World people are those from developing countries where poverty is often a problem.

Jones wrote the musical score for the film version of *The Color Purple*. He was also appointed to work with Walker. His job was to look out for Walker's interests—to make sure that no one made any changes in the story that would embarrass her or the African-American community.

On the same day that Alice Walker received the Pulitzer Prize for *The Color Purple*, actress/comedian Whoopi Goldberg bought the book. After reading it, Goldberg wrote to Walker and asked her to let her play Celie. Goldberg was performing her comedy routine in nightclubs then. She had never done a movie and was not well known. However, Walker was familiar with Goldberg's work. When Quincy Jones asked Walker whom she wanted to play Celie, she said Goldberg.

Goldberg said that she thought singer Tina Turner would be a good choice for the part of Shug Avery. Jones and Spielberg offered Turner the part, but she refused it. The role went to actress Margaret Avery. She earned the part when she showed up at the audition looking very "Shug-ish" wearing a red ostrich feather. The fact that her last name was the same as her character's was only a coincidence.

Spielberg and Jones selected Danny Glover as "Mister." Everyone involved with the planning of the movie agreed that Glover was excellent in the part.

Jones made another casting decision when he was in Chicago. He happened to turn on the television and saw a talk show hostess named Oprah Winfrey. She was popular in the Chicago area, but she did not yet have the name recognition she enjoys today. Nor did she have the acting experience. Still, Jones believed Winfrey was right for the part of Sophia, the wife of Celie's stepson Harpo.

Quincy Jones had assured Walker that she would be consulted throughout the filming of the movie. Walker actually spent time on the set during production and had input about decisions such as dialogue and clothing, which was an unusual arrangement. Normally, writers have no control over what a movie company does with their books.

Whoopie Goldberg read *The Color Purple* and liked it so much that she wrote to Alice Walker saying that she would like to play the part of Celie in the movie.

The completed movie later received eleven Academy Award nominations, including one for Best Picture. However, it did not come up a winner, losing to *Out of Africa.*

In a review of the movie for *Newsweek,* David Ansen said, "It's hard not to be moved by Spielberg's *Color Purple.*" On the other hand, he criticized parts of the film saying, "sometimes the sentimentality quotient is allowed to reach dangerously toxic levels."[14]

However, most of the criticism of the movie came from African-American men who felt there were no good male role models in the story. They were especially outraged by the character of "Mister."

The criticism hurt Walker. She felt that she had been misunderstood.[15] Walker finally answered her critics in an essay published in *Ms.* magazine in the November 1986 issue. She agreed that at the beginning of the book "Mister" was mean and oppressed women. But she liked him, because he had the courage to change.

"It is a mistake to assume that Celie's 'meekness' makes her a saint and Mister's brutality makes him a devil," Walker wrote. "The point is, neither of these people is healthy."[16] Then Walker explained how they both changed. Celie became more "self-interested and aggressive"; "Mister" became more "thoughtful and considerate of others."

It is this ability to change that interests Walker. It is why she calls herself an optimist. She says she saw a revolution in the South. For her, it was an indication of how much people and society can change.

Walker's second collection of essays *Living by the Word* was published in 1988. It is a collection of essays, letters, and lectures written between 1973 and 1987. It also includes journal entries from her years in California.

Reviewers have called *Living by the Word* Walker's most "spiritual" writing. Walker herself said that by this time she had come to understand her work as prayer.[17]

The title came from a dream Walker had. In the dream she was visited by a two-headed woman. Walker interpreted the women to be an African American, a Native American, or anyone who was "different." The woman was giving advice to people. Since Walker was concerned about the environment, she asked the woman if the world would survive. The woman said "No." Then Walker asked what she could do. The woman answered, "Live by the word and keep on walking."[18]

Walker called this book a "journey."[19] It is a journey in both the physical and spiritual sense. The physical journey includes essays about her travels to China, Bali, and Jamaica. The spiritual journey includes memories of family and friends, her insights about the criticism directed at *The Color Purple*, her concerns about human rights and the environment, and changes in her own life.

"My Big Brother Bill" is about her Native American friend Bill Wahpepah. In that essay, Walker wrote about a period in her life when she immersed herself in the

Alice Walker has been nurtured by the beauty, silence, and peace of nature.

Native American culture. She studied Cherokee folklore and surrounded herself with Native American art, rugs, and jewelry.

"Am I Blue?" describes the pain a horse suffered when his mate was taken away from him. Writing that essay led to Walker's decision to become a vegetarian. She began to see eating meat as cannibalism. She wrote more about that decision in another essay titled "Why Did the Balinese Chicken Cross the Road?" Walker admits that she occasionally eats meat, but most of the time avoids it.

In a journal entry, Walker told about protesting the shipment of arms to Central America in 1987. Walker and others were arrested when they attempted to block a gate of the Concord Naval Weapons Station in California.

The arrest was not something new for Walker. She is known as a political activist. She once said that her activism "pays the rent on being alive."[20] Walker regrets that she does not have the energy to get as politically involved as she would like. "If I had the energy that goes along with my feelings of commitment . . . I would be arrested almost every week,"[21] she told an interviewer.

In a review for *Library Journal*, Mollie Brodsky called *Living by the Word* "entertaining and often stirring."[22] Author Donna Haisty Winchell noted Walker's sincerity but said that sometimes Walker "looks rather foolish and eccentric."[23] An example she gave was an essay called

Alice Walker with the rewards of her gardening.

"Everything Is a Human Being." In this essay Walker tried to imagine how she would feel about human beings if she were a tree.

Although Winchell thought Walker looked foolish in this instance, Noel Perrin, in *The New York Times Book Review*, called the essay a "success." He also said that different readers would see different things in the book. "It will depend heavily on who you are,"[24] he wrote.

Walker spent eight years working on her fourth novel, *Temple of My Familiar*. It was published in 1989. Walker described the book as "a romance of the last 500,000 years."[25] In it she brought back some of the characters from *The Color Purple*, including Shug and Celie. In fact, Walker says that the reason she started writing it was because she missed them.[26]

The story centers around three marriages. There is Arveyda, a popular musician, and his wife Carlotta, who is a Latin-American refugee and a professor of women's literature. The second couple is Suwelo, a history professor who has an affair with Carlotta, and his wife Fanny. Fanny is the granddaughter of Celie. She is a professor of women's studies who leaves teaching to become a masseuse. Mr. Hal and Miss Lissie are an elderly couple who become friends with Suwelo after the death of his Uncle Rafe.

The story takes place in America, England, Africa, and Latin America. It weaves back and forth in place and time as the characters tell about their lives and the lives of their ancestors. The setting is further expanded through Miss Lissie who has memories of many previous lives, including one as an African pygmy.

The book received mixed reviews. Some praised Walker's ability to create interesting characters. Ursula K. LeGuin of *The San Francisco Review of Books* said, "All the people are passionate actors and sufferers."[27] In a review for *Library Journal,* Jessica Grim called the characters "magnetic."[28]

However, others were critical of Walker's use of history. In a review for *Time* magazine, Paul Gray wrote, "Parts of it are enchantingly beautiful. . . . But when Walker's characters venture into more recent history, their opinions to put it discreetly, seem open to debate."[29]

James Wolcott of the *New Republic* called the book "the nuttiest novel I've ever read."[30]

Walker was philosophical about the negative criticism. "I *do* understand that my worldview is different from that of most of the critics,"[31] she said. "I can only persist in being myself."[32]

10

A Delicate Subject

Walker's fifth book of poetry *Her Blue Body Everything We Know* was published in 1991. It is a collection of her first four poetry books, plus sixteen new poems. The title is a line from one of the new poems called "We Have a Beautiful Mother." The poem personifies the earth, giving it the human characteristics of a mother.

When she was working on this collection, Walker says that she had the urge to rewrite some of her poems. She did not, however, because she realized they were like a journal. The poems showed how she felt at the time she wrote them. "I like leaving a record of the way I was rather than a record that has been improved upon,"[1] she said.

Adrian T. Oktenbery of *Women's Review of Books* said, "*Her Blue Body* reflects the inner journey of an extraordinary writer over 25 years of struggle. It teaches us . . . to cherish and celebrate life."[2]

Walker's second picture book *Finding the Green Stone* was also published in 1991. It was the first book she had actually written as a picture book. Her first picture book *To Hell With Dying* was originally published as a short story.

Finding the Green Stone tells the story of two children, Johnny and Katie, who live in a town where everyone has a stone that glows with a green light. Then Johnny has a bad day. He calls his neighbor a name and says mean things to his parents. He also loses his stone. Is it just a coincidence that the stone disappears at a time when Johnny is being spiteful? As the story unfolds, the children learn that it is the love in their hearts that makes the stone glow.

Critics agreed that Walker had good intentions in writing this book. However, they also thought she was too obvious about teaching a lesson. *Publishers Weekly* critiqued, "Walker presents a rather forced message in this strange story."[3] In a review for *School Library Journal*, Patricia Dooley wrote that she liked the illustrations done by Catherine Deeter, but was not impressed with the story. "Deeter's warm, bright acrylics are cheery and attractive, but can't save this tract from sinking under its own well-intentioned weight,"[4] she wrote.

The following year, in 1992, Walker's fifth novel *Possessing the Secret of Joy* was published. Walker says it took her a year to write the book after twenty-five years of thinking about it.[5] The novel is about female circumcision, which is also called clitoridectomy. Walker and other human rights activists refer to it as "female genital mutilation."[6]

The custom of female circumcision is widespread in the Middle East, Southeast Asia, and Africa. Recent figures indicate that an estimated 85 to 114 million women—mostly Muslims—have had this type of surgery.[7] There are also reported cases of female circumcision taking place in France, the United States, and other countries as people who believe in these practices immigrate to other areas.

Clitoridectomy is normally performed on girls twelve years old and younger—sometimes even on infants. Its purpose is to ensure virginity, intending to make the girls marriageable.

The circumciser (usually not a doctor) removes all or part of the external genitalia. In some cases, the vulva is actually stitched closed, leaving only a small opening for urination and menstruation. The surgery is performed while the girls are awake and held down. They are not given anything for pain. The circumciser often uses crude tools and operates under unsanitary conditions.

Walker first heard about this practice when she was in college. It took her the next twenty-five years to figure out how to write about it. "I dragged my feet for a long time, because I knew my whole life would change once I

Alice Walker at her country home in 1992.

published it," Walker says. "But I could not continue going on blithely, as if this weren't happening."[8]

Walker went to Mexico to write the novel. She wanted to understand what it would be like to have major surgery in a third-world country without the aid of anesthetics or antiseptics.

The book tells the story of Tashi who first appeared in *The Color Purple*. However, Walker does not call this book a sequel. "I hate sequels,"[9] she says. However, she does believe that sometimes there are characters who need to be more fully developed.[10] Tashi was one of those characters.

In *The Color Purple*, Celie's two babies are taken from her at birth. They are adopted by a young missionary couple who are sent to Africa. By a twist of fate, Celie's sister Nettie is hired by the family and travels to Africa with them.

Tashi is the young African girl with whom Celie's son Adam falls in love. Because of the influence of the missionaries, Tashi did not have the traditional circumcision as a girl. She feels this makes her an "outsider" in her tribe. When Adam goes to London with his family, she has the surgery.

Adam returns and he and Tashi get married and move to the United States. Tashi struggles to find happiness in her new life, but she is haunted by the past. Her sister Dura was circumcised as a child. She bled to death as a result of the surgery. Her sister's death and her own surgery have left Tashi with deep physical and emotional scars. Tashi's only child, a son, suffers brain damage at birth—a direct result of her circumcision. Tashi returns to Africa and confronts her circumciser. When the woman dies under mysterious circumstances, Tashi is accused of murdering her.

Using fiction to make a political statement is hard. The author sometimes concentrates too much on the message, and consequently, the story suffers. Reviewers disagreed about how successful Walker was at combining politics and fiction in this book.

Publishers Weekly critiqued, "Walker's protest against 'what men . . . do to us' cannot be faulted; it's guise as a novel, however, can."[11] On the other hand, Laura Shapiro who wrote for *Newsweek*, called the book "a true rarity: a novel that's strengthened, not strangled, by its political mission."[12]

Before Walker's book was published, only a few women had spoken against female circumcision. There had been no large-scale organized effort to end the practice. Through her novel, Walker was able to give the issue widespread attention. But still she did not think she had done enough. She decided to make a documentary film about female circumcision.

Walker contacted Pratibha Parmar, a London-based filmmaker. Parmar had made several other documentaries and Walker admired her work. Walker used her advance from the publisher of *Possessing the Secret of Joy* to help finance the project. Although the amount of the advance was undisclosed, it was reported to be a six-figure number.[13]

Parmar and Walker traveled to England and Africa to film. They interviewed women who performed the circumcisions and women who had undergone the procedure. They also focused on the cultural background of the practice.

The film, called *Warrior Marks*, was first shown in the United States on November 3, 1993. The debut took place in New York City.

Walker and Parmar also wrote a companion book. During the making of the film, they both kept journals of their experiences. Later they compiled their journals, transcripts from the interviews they conducted, and photos taken during filming. The result was a book titled *Warrior Marks: Female Genital Mutilation and the Sexual Blinding of Women*, which was released on November 1, 1993.

Walker was afraid western women would see female circumcision as "foolish." She made it clear that westerners had peculiar customs as well. She compared female circumcision to breast enlargement, starving to reach some "ideal" weight, and even the straightening of hair by African-American women.[14]

Public opinion about the book and the movie was divided. On one side were those who believed female circumcision was a violation of human rights. They

Alice Walker with filmmaker Pratibha Parmar. Together they wrote *Warrior Marks: Female Genital Mutilation and the Sexual Blinding of Women.*

wanted to put an end to the practice. On the other side were those who felt people needed to be tolerant of the customs of others.

A. M. Rosenthal, a columnist for the *New York Times*, joined Walker in speaking against female circumcision. Rosenthal called clitoridectomy "the world's most widespread form of torture"[15] and urged the United Nations to get involved to put an end to the practice.

Wilkista Onsando, a women's rights leader in Kenya, Africa, did not want interference from other countries. She said the women of Africa should be allowed to fight against this practice in their own manner. "It will die faster than if others tell us what to do."[16]

Female circumcision was banned by the Kenyan government in 1990. Yet it is still widely practiced there. Walker felt that she could not be patient. "Torture is not culture,"[17] she said.

Dr. Nahid Toubia, a Sudanese surgeon, accused Walker of using the topic to revive a fading writing career. "This is a very sensitive issue that she's trying to sensationalize in order to get the limelight back,"[18] Toubia said.

Walker knew that many people would not agree with what she had to say about female circumcision. She hoped that they would use what they saw in the film as a starting point to explore their own feelings about this delicate subject.[19]

All the media attention on female circumcision has proved that Walker did what she wanted to do—made people think. It is what she tries to do with all her writing. Walker does not let her readers just sit back and enjoy her books. She forces them to look at problems they might not have to deal with otherwise. "Sometimes what people need is just to see how you see it from your angle,"[20] she said.

Through her writing, Walker has acquired a huge following of loyal fans. Her friend Gloria Steinem once wrote about a trip she took with Walker in the early 1970s.[21] They had gone to Atlanta, Georgia, for a march to celebrate Martin Luther King, Jr.'s birthday. Steinem lost Walker in the crowd. While she was searching for Walker, she met a group of students from Spelman College. They were also looking for Walker, hoping to get a chance to meet her. They had read all her books. They had even gone to Eatonton to see her childhood home. They wanted to know everything about the writer who meant so much to them.[22]

A woman who had spent her life fighting for equal rights once explained why Walker's writing was so important to her. The woman said:

> She's certainly not the only writer who sees personal cruelty and social injustice clearly. But she's the only writer I know who sees it all: what happens to black people here, to women everywhere; the outrages against history and the

earth; everything. Yet she has taught me that cruelty turns back on itself—which gives me faith to keep on fighting.[23]

There is no reason to think that the criticism aimed at Walker for *Warrior Marks* or any of her other books will keep her from writing what needs to be said. She has faced critics in the past and persevered. As long as there is injustice in the world, she will continue to fight against it.

Chronology

1944—Born in Eatonton, Georgia, on February 9.

1961—Graduated high school; received a scholarship to attend Spelman College.

1963—Transferred to Sarah Lawrence College.

1964—Traveled through Africa and Europe.

1965—Awarded a B.A. degree from Sarah Lawrence College; moved to New York City; worked with the New York City Welfare Department.

1966—Received her first writing grant; went to Mississippi to write.

1967—Received a fellowship to the MacDowell Colony; married Mel Leventhal on March 17; moved to Mississippi; became a consultant for a Headstart program called Friends of the Children of Mississippi.

1968—Attended Dr. Martin Luther King, Jr.'s, funeral in Atlanta, Georgia; became writer-in-residence at Jackson State University; her first poetry collection *Once* was published.

1969—Daughter Rebecca was born.

1970—Became writer-in-residence at Tougaloo College; first novel *The Third Life of Grange Copeland* was published.

1972—Moved to Cambridge, Massachusetts; taught at Wellesley College and then at the University of Massachusetts in Boston.

1973—*Revolutionary Petunias and Other Poems* was published; first short story collection *In Love and Trouble: Stories of Black Women* was published.

1974—Moved back to New York; became a contributing editor at *Ms.* magazine; *Langston Hughes: American Poet* was published.

1976—Divorced Mel Leventhal; *Meridian* was published.

1978—Moved to San Francisco.

1979—Published *Goodnight, Willie Lee, I'll See You in the Morning* and *I Love Myself When I Am Laughing . . . and Then Again When I Am Looking Mean and Impressive.*

1981—Second book of short stories, *You Can't Keep a Good Woman Down*, was published.

1982—*The Color Purple* was published; became a professor at the University of California, Berkeley (spring) and Brandeis University (fall).

1983—First collection of essays, *In Search of Our Mothers' Gardens: Womanist Prose* was published.

1984—*Horses Make a Landscape Look More Beautiful* was published; begins Wild Trees Press with Robert Allen.

1986—Premiere for the movie *The Color Purple* in Eatonton, Georgia, on January 18.

1988—*To Hell with Dying* was published as a children's book; *Living by the Word* was published.

1989—*The Temple of My Familiar* was published.

1991—*Finding the Green Stone* and *Her Blue Body Everything We Know: Earthling Poems 1965–1990 Complete* was published.

1992—*Possessing the Secret of Joy* was published.

1993—*Warrior Marks: Female Genital Mutilation and the Sexual Blinding of Women* was published; the film *Warrior Marks* made its U.S. debut.

Chapter Notes

Chapter 1

1. "Alice Walker Goes Home to Eatonton, Ga., for 'Color Purple' Premiere," *Jet*, February 10, 1986, p. 30.

2. Don Schanche, Jr., "Town Welcomes Favorite Daughter," *Macon Telegraph and News*, January 19, 1986, p. C1.

3. Peter S. Prescott, "A Long Road to Liberation," *Newsweek*, June 21, 1982, p. 67.

4. "Books," *The New Yorker*, September 6, 1982, p. 106.

5. Claudia Dreifus, "Alice Walker 'Writing to Save My Life'," *The Progressive*, August 1989, p. 29.

6. Ibid.

7. "Seeing Red Over Purple," *People Weekly*, March 10, 1986, p. 102.

8. Ibid.

9. Ibid.

10. Alice Walker, *Living by the Word: Selected Writings 1973–1987* (San Diego: Harcourt Brace Jovanovich, 1988), p. 109.

Chapter 2

1. Alice Walker, *In Search of Our Mothers' Gardens: Womanist Prose* (San Diego: Harcourt Brace Jovanovich, 1983), p. 21.

2. Alvin P. Sanoff, "The Craft of Survival," *U.S. News & World Report*, June 3, 1991, p. 51.

3. Ibid.

4. *The Originals: Alice Walker*, videocassette, SNJ Productions, 1988.

5. Alice Walker, *Living by the Word: Selected Writings 1973–1987* (San Diego: Harcourt Brace Jovanovich, 1988), p. 13.

6. Ibid.

7. Ibid.

8. Gregory Jaynes, "Living by the Word," *Life*, May 1989, p. 62.

9. Ibid.

10. Walker, *In Search of Our Mothers' Gardens*, p. 385.

11. Ibid., p. 386.

12. Ibid.

13. Ibid.

14. Gloria Steinem, "Do You Know This Woman? She Knows You: A Profile of Alice Walker," *Ms.*, June 1982, p. 92.

15. Ibid.

16. *In Black and White: Part 4*, videocassette, California Newsreel, 1992.

17. Ibid.

18. Steinem, p. 92.

Chapter 3

1. Alice Walker, *In Search of Our Mothers' Gardens: Womanist Prose* (San Diego: Harcourt Brace Jovanovich, 1983), p. 390.

2. Walker, p. 124.

3. Mary Helen Washington, "Alice Walker: Her Mother's Gifts," *Ms.*, June 1982, p. 38.

4. Ibid.

5. Ibid.

6. Walker, p. 163.

Chapter 4

1. *The Originals: Alice Walker*, videocassette, SNJ Productions, 1988.

2. Alice Walker, *In Search of Our Mothers' Gardens: Womanist Prose* (San Diego: Harcourt Brace Jovanovich, 1983), p. 146.

3. Ibid., p. 161.

4. Ibid., p. 130.

5. Gloria Steinem, "Do You Know This Woman? She Knows You: A Profile of Alice Walker," *Ms.*, June 1982, p. 93.

6. Walker, *In Search of Our Mothers' Gardens*, p. 245.

7. Ibid.

8. Donna Haisty Winchell, *Alice Walker* (New York: Twayne Publishers, 1992), p. 7.

9. Gregory Jaynes, "Living by the Word," *Life*, May 1989, p. 62.

10. Walker, *In Search of Our Mothers' Gardens*, p. 245.

11. Ibid., p. 248.

12. Ibid., p. 247.

13. Ibid., p. 263.

14. Ibid., p. 248.

15. Estelle Benedict, "The Book Review," *Library Journal*, September 15, 1968, p. 3145.

16. Charles Moritz, ed., *Current Biography Yearbook* 1984 (New York: The H. W. Wilson Company, 1984), p. 431.

17. Walker, *In Search of Our Mothers' Gardens*, p. 248.

18. Ibid., p. 254.

19. Alice Walker, *In Love & Trouble: Stories of Black Women* (San Diego: Harcourt Brace Jovanovich, 1973), p. 129.

20. Alice Walker, *Living by the Word: Selected Writings 1973–1987* (San Diego: Harcourt Brace Jovanovich, 1988), p. 38.

21. Ibid.

22. Ibid., p. 40.

Chapter 5

1. Alice Walker, *In Search of Our Mothers' Gardens: Womanist Prose* (San Diego: Harcourt Brace Jovanovich, 1983), p. 135.

2. Ibid., p. 224.

3. Ibid., p. 163.

4. Alice Walker, *The Third Life of Grange Copeland* (New York: Pocket Books, 1970), p. 342.

5. Walker, *In Search of Our Mothers' Gardens*, p. 28.

6. Ibid., p. 192.

7. Ibid., p. 224.

8. Ibid.

9. Claudia Dreifus, "Alice Walker 'Writing to Save My Life'," *The Progressive*, August 1989, p. 29.

10. Walker, *In Search of Our Mothers' Gardens*, p. 224.

11. Ibid., p. 147.

12. Ibid., p. 148.

13. Ibid., p. 149.

14. Dreifus, p. 30.

15. Alvin P. Sanoff, "The Craft of Survival," *U.S. News & World Report*, June 3, 1991, p. 51.

16. Josephine Hendin, "SR: Books," *Saturday Review*, August 22, 1970, p. 56.

17. Robert Coles, "Books: To Try Men's Souls," *New Yorker*, February 27, 1971, p. 106.

18. David Bradley, "Telling the Black Woman's Story," *The New York Times Magazine*, January 8, 1984, p. 36.

19. *The Originals: Alice Walker*, videocassette, SNJ Productions, 1988.

Chapter 6

1. Alice Walker, *In Search of Our Mothers' Gardens: Womanist Prose* (San Diego: Harcourt Brace Jovanovich, 1983), p. 135.

2. Ibid., p. 9.

3. Ibid., p. 12.

4. Ibid., p. 83.

5. Ibid., p. 86.

6. Alice Walker, ed., *I Love Myself When I Am Laughing . . . And Then Again When I Am Looking Mean and Impressive* (New York: The Feminist Press, 1979), p. 1.

7. Walker, *In Search of Our Mothers' Gardens*, p. 224.

8. Ibid., p. 225.

9. Ibid., p. 107.

10. Walker, *I Love Myself When I am Laughing . . . And Then Again When I'm Looking Mean and Impressive*, p. i.

Chapter 7

1. Alice Walker, *In Search of Our Mothers' Gardens: Womanist Prose* (San Diego: Harcourt Brace Jovanovich, 1983), p. 268.

2. Alice Walker, *Her Blue Body Everything We Know: Earthling Poems 1965–1990 Complete* (San Diego: Harcourt Brace Jovanovich, 1991), p. 154.

3. Alice Walker, *In Love and Trouble: Stories of Black Women* (San Diego: Harcourt Brace Jovanovich, 1973), p. 87.

4. Ibid., p. 4.

5. Ibid., p. 120.

6. Mel Watkins, *The New York Times Book Review*, March 17, 1974, p. 41.

7. Barbara Smith, "The Souls of Black Women," *Ms.*, February 1974, p. 43.

8. Henry Louis Gates, Jr., and K. A. Appiah, eds., *Alice Walker: Critical Perspectives Past and Present* (New York: Amistad Press, Inc., 1993), p. 206.

9. Ibid., p. 325.

10. Gregory Jaynes, "Living by the Word," *Life*, May 1989, p. 64.

11. Gates, p. 11.

12. "Books Briefly," *The Progressive*, October 1976, p. 60.

13. Gordon Burnside, "Books," *Commonweal*, April 29, 1977, p. 284.

14. Walker, *Her Blue Body Everything We Know: Earthling Poems 1965-1990 Complete*, p. 239.

15. Ibid., p. 307.

16. Alice Walker, *Living by the Word: Selected Writings 1973–1987* (San Diego: Harcourt Brace Jovanovich, 1988), p. 9.

17. Walker, *In Search of Our Mothers' Gardens*, p. 216.

18. Ibid.

19. Walker, *Living by the Word*, p. 10.

Chapter 8

1. Alice Walker, *In Search of Our Mothers' Gardens: Womanist Prose* (San Diego: Harcourt Brace Jovanovich, 1983), p. 355.

2. Ibid.

3. Gloria Steinem, "Do You Know This Woman? She Knows You: A Profile of Alice Walker," *Ms.*, June 1982, p. 90.

4. Walker, *In Search of Our Mothers' Gardens*, p. 356.

5. Ibid.

6. Steinem, p. 90.

7. Walker, *In Search of Our Mothers' Gardens*, p. 359.

8. Steinem, p. 90.

9. Walker, *In Search of Our Mothers' Gardens*, p. 360.

10. Henry Louis Gates, Jr., and K. A. Appiah, eds., *Alice Walker: Critical Perspectives Past and Present* (New York: Amistad, 1993), p. 319.

11. Steinem, p. 89.

12. Ibid.

13. Alice Walker, *The Color Purple* (New York: Washington Square Press, 1982), p. 19.

14. Ibid., p. 50.

15. Gates, p. 320.

16. Ibid., p. 18.

17. Steinem, p. 89.

18. Walker, *The Color Purple*, p. 193.

19. *The Originals: Alice Walker*, videocassette, SNJ Productions, 1988.

20. *In Black and White: Part 4*, videocassette, California Newsreel, 1992.

21. Ibid.

22. Jacqueline Trescott, "A Child of the South, a Writer of the Heart," *The Washington Post*, August 8, 1976, p. G3.

23. Ibid.

Chapter 9

1. Alice Walker, *Her Blue Body Everything We Know: Earthling Poems 1965–1990 Complete* (San Diego: Harcourt Brace Jovanovich, 1991), p. 311.

2. Ibid.

3. Ibid., p. 315.

4. Ibid., p. 370.

5. Ibid., p. 329.

6. Alice Walker, *Living by the Word: Selected Writings 1973–1987* (San Diego: Harcourt Brace Jovanovich, 1988), p. 82.

7. Andrea Fleck Clardy, "Best-Sellers from Crone's Own, Light Cleaning, Down There and Dozens of Other Feminist Presses," *Ms.*, August 1985, p. 68.

8. Pat Rose, "Growing Books at Wild Trees Press," *Small Press*, November/December 1986, p. 35.

9. Susan Dworkin, "The Making of *The Color Purple*," *Ms.*, December 1985, p. 68.

10. Ibid.

11. Ibid.

12. Ray Anello, "Characters in Search of a Book," *Newsweek*, June 21, 1982, p. 67.

13. Dworkin, p. 70.

14. David Ansen, "We Shall Overcome: Spielberg Takes on Rural, Matriarchal Black Life," *Newsweek*, December 30, 1985, p. 59.

15. Gregory Jaynes, "Living by the Word," *Life*, May 1989, p. 62.

16. Alice Walker, *Living by the Word: Selected Writings* 1973–1987 (San Diego: Harcourt Brace Jovanovich, 1988), p. 80.

17. Ibid., p. 47.

18. Ibid., p. 2.

19. Ibid., p. xx.

20. Claudia Dreifus, "Alice Walker 'Writing to Save My Life,'" *The Progressive*, August 1989, p. 30.

21. *The Originals: Alice Walker*, videocassette, SNJ Productions, 1988.

22. Mollie Brodsky, "Book Review," *Library Journal*, May 1, 1988, p. 81.

23. Donna Haisty Winchell, *Alice Walker* (New York: Twayne Publishers, 1992), p. 7.

24. Noel Perrin, "Another Sojourner," *The New York Times Book Review*, June 5, 1988, p. 42.

25. Gregory Jaynes, "Living by the Word," *Life*, May 1989, p. 64.

26. Ibid.

27. Henry Louis Gates, Jr., and K. A. Appiah, eds., *Alice Walker: Critical Perspectives Past and Present* (New York: Amistad, 1993), p. 22.

28. Jessica Grim, "Book Reviews," *Library Journal*, March 15, 1989, p. 88.

29. Paul Gray, "A Myth To Be Taken on Faith," *Time*, May 1, 1989, p. 69.

30. James Wolcott, "Party of Animals," *New Republic*, May 29, 1989, p. 28.

31. Dreifus, p. 29.

32. Ibid.

Chapter 10

1. Alvin P. Sanoff, "The Craft of Survival," *U.S. News & World Report*, June 3, 1991, p. 51.

2. Adrian T. Oktenbery, *Women's Review of Books*, December 1991, p. 24.

3. "Forecasts," *Publishers Weekly*, October 25, 1991, p. 66.

4. Patricia Dooley, "Book Review," *School Library Journal*, February 1992, p. 79.

5. Alice Walker and Pratibha Parmar, *Warrior Marks: Female Genital Mutilation and the Sexual Blinding of Women* (New York: Harcourt Brace Jovanovich, 1993), p. 269.

6. David A. Kaplan, "Is It Torture or Tradition?" *Newsweek*, December 20, 1993, p. 124.

7. Ibid.

8. Paula Giddings, "Alice Walker's Appeal," *Essence*, July 1992, p. 60.

9. Charles Whitaker, "Alice Walker: *Color Purple* Author Confronts Her Critics and Talks About Her Provocative New Book," *Ebony*, May 1992, p. 88.

10. Ibid.

11. "Forecasts," *Publishers Weekly*, April 13, 1992, p. 41.

12. Laura Shapiro, "The Books of Summer," *Newsweek*, June 8, 1992, p. 57.

13. Maureen O'Brien, "Alice Walker Offers a New Book and a Film—With a Cause," *Publishers Weekly*, October 25, 1993, p. 13.

14. Walker and Parmar, *Warrior Marks*, pp. 9–10; pp. 13-14.

15. Kaplan, p. 124.

16. Ibid.

17. Ibid.

18. Ibid.

19. Walker and Parmar, *Warrior Marks*, p. 281.

20. *The Originals: Alice Walker*, videocassette, SNJ Productions, 1988.

21. Gloria Steinem, "Do You Know This Woman? She Knows You: A Profile of Alice Walker," *Ms.*, June 1982, p. 94.

22. Ibid.

23. Ibid., p. 37.

Further Reading

Bradley, David. "Telling the Black Woman's Story." *The New York Times Magazine.* August 8, 1984, pp. 25–37.

Dreifus, Claudia. "Alice Walker 'Writing to Save My Life.'" *The Progressive.* August 1989, pp. 29–31.

Dworkin, Susan. "The Making of *The Color Purple*." *Ms.* December 1985, pp. 66–70.

Gates, Henry Louis, Jr., and K. A. Appiah, eds. *Alice Walker: Critical Perspectives Past and Present.* New York: Amistad Press, 1993.

Giddings, Paula. "Alice Walker's Appeal." *Essence.* July 1992, pp. 59–62.

Jaynes, Gregory. "Living by the Word." *Life.* May 1989, pp. 61–64.

Kaplan, David A. "Is It Torture or Tradition?" *Newsweek.* December 20, 1993, p. 124.

O'Brien, Maureen. "Alice Walker Offers a New Book and a Film—With a Cause." *Publishers Weekly.* October 25, 1993, p. 13.

Sanoff, Alvin P. "The Craft of Survival." *U.S. News & World Report.* June 3, 1991, p. 51.

Steinem, Gloria. "Do You Know This Woman? She Knows You: A Profile of Alice Walker." *Ms.* June 1982, pp. 36–37.

Trescott, Jacqueline. "A Child of the South, a Writer of the Heart." *The Washington Post.* August 8, 1976, p. G1.

Washington, Mary Helen. "Alice Walker: Her Mother's Gifts." *Ms.* June 1982, p. 38.

Whitaker, Charles. "Alice Walker: *Color Purple* Author Confronts Her Critics and Talks About Her Provocative New Book." *Ebony.* May 1992, pp. 85–90.

Winchell, Donna Haisty. *Alice Walker.* New York: Twayne Publishers, 1992.

Videocassettes

In Black and White: Part 4. California Newsreel, 1992.

The Originals: Alice Walker. SNJ Productions, 1988.

Index

A

Academy Awards, 93
Allen, Robert, 75, 78, 88
American Book Award, 8
American Institute of Arts and
    Letters, 67
Ansen, David, 93
Avery, Margaret, 91

B

Benedict, Estelle, 36
Bradley, David, 51
Brandeis University, 81
Brodsky, Mollie, 96
Burnside, Gordon, 70

C

Caldwell, Earl, 9
Civil Rights Movement,
    24-25, 35-38, 41-44,
    67-70, 82
Coles, Robert, 50-51
Cuban Missile Crisis, 29

D

Dabbs, Bill, 7
Deeter, Catherine, 102
Dooley, Patricia, 102
Dreifus, Claudia, 47

G

Glover, Danny, 9-11, 91
Goldberg, Whoopi, 90-92
Gray, Paul, 99
Grim, Jessica, 99
Guber, Peter, 88-89

H

Hendin, Josephine, 50

Hughes, Langston, 39, 67
Hurston, Zora Neale, 55-62,
    79, 82

J

Jackson State University, 48
Jaynes, Gregory, 73
Jones, Quincy, 89-91

K

Kennedy, John F., 29-30, 32
King, Coretta Scott, 30, 47
King, Martin Luther, Jr.,
    24-25, 30, 32-33, 44,
    46-47, 82, 110

L

LeGuin, Ursula K., 99
Leventhal, Mel, 42-47, 49, 70
Lillian Smith Award, 65

M

MacDowell Colony, New
    Hampshire, 44-45
Montgomery Improvement
    Association, 25
Morehouse College, 75
Mueller, Lisel, 36

O

Oktenbery, Adrian T.,
    101-102
Onsando, Wilkista, 109

P

Parks, Rosa, 24-25
Parmar, Pratibha, 106-108
Perrin, Noel, 98
Peters, Jon, 88-89
Pulitzer Prize, 8, 90

R

Richard and Hinda Rosenthal
   Award, 67
Rosenthal, A. M., 109
Rukeyser, Muriel, 35-39

S

Sanoff, Alvin P., 14
Sarah Lawrence College, 34,
   37, 41
Shapiro, Laura, 106
Smith, Barbara, 67
Spelman College, 28-34, 43,
   66, 75, 110
Spielberg, Steven, 88-91
Steinem, Gloria, 75, 80, 110
Student Nonviolent Coordinating
   Committee (SNCC), 32

T

Toubia, Nahid, 109
Tougaloo College, 48

U

University of California,
   Berkeley, 81
University of Massachusetts,
   59-60

V

Van Vechten, Carl, 57, 62

W

Walker, Alice
   books of
      Color Purple, The, 5-6,
         8-9, 11, 73-82, 94,
         98, 105
      Finding the Green Stone,
         102
      Good Night, Willie Lee,
         I'll See You in the
         Morning, 71, 74

Her Blue Body
   Everything We Know,
   101-102
Horses Make a
   Landscape More
   Beautiful, 85-88
I Love Myself When I
   Am Laughing...and
   Then Again When I
   Am Looking Mean
   and Impressive, 60-62
In Love and Trouble:
   Stories of Black
   Women, 65-67
In Search of Our Mother's
   Gardens: Womanist
   Prose, 82-84
Langston Hughes:
   American Poet, 67
Living by the Word, 94-98
Meridian, 67-70
Once, 35-38
Possessing the Secret of
   Joy, 102-107
Revolutionary Petunias and
   Other Poems, 64-65
Temple of My Familiar,
   The, 98-99
Third Life of Grange
   Copeland, The, 48-52
To Hell With Dying,
   38-39, 102
Warrior Marks: Female
   Genital Mutilation
   and the Sexual
   Blinding of Women,
   107-111

You Can't Keep a Good Woman Down, 76

childhood, 6, 13-28, 82

college, 28-39

films of

Color Purple, The, 5-7, 9-11, 88-93

Warrior Marks, 106-107

marriage and divorce, 45-47, 49, 59, 67, 70

motherhood, 48-49, 59, 70, 74, 76-78, 83, 90

on activism, 81-82, 96

on criticism of her work, 6-11, 51-52, 93, 99, 109-110

on her ancestors, 51, 84, 87-88

on the environment, 86-87, 94

on vegetarianism, 96

on writing, 47-48, 51-52, 73-74, 94

siblings, 6-7, 13, 16, 18-20, 23, 34-35, 64-65

Walker, Minnie Tallulah ("Lou"), 14-15, 26-27, 35, 53-54, 63-64, 84

Walker, Willie Lee, 13, 15-16, 34-35, 71

Watkins, Mel, 66-67, 80

Wellesley College, 59-61

Wild Trees Press, 88

Winchell, Donna Haisty, 96-98

Winfrey, Oprah, 9-11, 91

Wolcott, James, 99

World Youth Peace Festival, 30